The Same Sex Controversy

BHP BOOKS BY JAMES R. WHITE

The Forgotten Trinity
The God Who Justifies
Grieving: Our Path Back to Peace
Is the Mormon My Brother?
The King James Only Controversy
Letters to a Mormon Elder
Mary—Another Redeemer?
The Roman Catholic Controversy
*What's With the Dudes at the Door?**
*What's With the Mutant in the Microscope?**

*with Kevin Johnson

Defending and Clarifying the Bible's
Message About Homosexuality

THE SAME SEX CONTROVERSY

JAMES R. WHITE
& JEFFREY D. NIELL

BETHANY HOUSE PUBLISHERS
Minneapolis, Minnesota

Published by Bethany House Publishers
A Ministry of Bethany Fellowship International
11400 Hampshire Avenue South
Bloomington, Minnesota 55438
www.bethanyhouse.com

Printed in the United States of America by
Bethany Press International, Bloomington, Minnesota 55438

Library of Congress Cataloging-in-Publication Data

White, James R. (James Robert), 1962-
    The same sex controversy : defending and clarifying the Bible's
message about homosexuality / by James R. White & Jeffrey D. Niell.
        p. cm.
Includes bibliographical references.
    ISBN 0-7642-2524-3 (pbk.)
    1. Homosexuality—Biblical teaching. 2. Homosexuality—Religious
aspects—Christianity. I. Niell, Jeffrey D. II. Title.
    BS680.H67 W47   2002
    241'.66—dc21   2002000912

This book is dedicated, with thankfulness, to the congregation of Emmanuel Covenant Church and in the hope that the church in our day will be strengthened to the glory of God. Let us never fear faithfulness to God's Word.

Jeffrey D. Niell

JAMES R. WHITE is the author of several acclaimed books, including *The God Who Justifies*, *The King James Only Controversy*, and *The Forgotten Trinity*. He is an elder of the Phoenix Reformed Baptist Church, director of Alpha and Omega Ministries—a Christian apologetics organization, adjunct professor with Golden Gate Baptist Theological Seminary, and professor of apologetics with Columbia Evangelical Seminary. He and his family live in Phoenix.

JEFFREY D. NIELL has an M.A. from Fuller Seminary. He is pastor of Emmanuel Covenant Church, a Presbyterian congregation in Phoenix, Arizona. He and his family make their home in Phoenix.

CONTENTS

CHAPTER ONE

The Unthinkable Has Become Thinkable

Our culture is inundated—in print and on screen—with the idea that homosexuality is a normal, proper, and healthy expression of "love" between persons. This view has successfully infiltrated our TV sitcoms, magazines, bookstores, and coffee shops, but now we are being told that homosexuality—in either orientation or act—is something approved by God and therefore consistent with biblical morality. The growing number of proponents of this view tell us that the Bible (rightly understood, interpreted, or translated) does not condemn homosexuality and that it even contains examples of loving, committed homosexual relationships within its pages. We are witnesses of a desperate clamor to move the authority of the Bible to the side of those who claim that homosexuality is an acceptable, God-approved lifestyle.

The call to receive homosexuality as a morally acceptable belief, or belief *and* behavior,[1] is now being heard in the church and by the church. The volume of this call is increasing as is the volume of books that are being produced. A proliferation of literature teaching this "new morality" under the guise of "right understanding" or "proper biblical interpretation" is resulting in the twisting of Scripture, the confusion of many, and the weakening of the church. With increasing vigor we are told that the previous ways are wrong and unenlightened. We are told that the Bible—previously thought to condemn homosexuality—does no such thing and that homosexuals (either in practice or merely in interest) need to be embraced by the church and allowed, if they so aspire, even to hold positions of authority in the church.

This push is evidence of a tragic cultural transformation that has occurred in recent decades—one that pertains to the ethical, to the moral, and to that which is right and wrong. Yesterday's outrage has become today's standard. Today, homosexuality, which at one time was morally unthinkable, is on parade before us as normal, acceptable, and—in order to show its authoritative status—unquestionable. Francis Schaeffer wrote,

> There is a "thinkable" and an "unthinkable" in every era. One era is quite certain intellectually and emotionally about what is acceptable. Yet another era decides that these "certainties" are unacceptable and puts another set of values into practice. On a humanistic base, people drift along from generation to generation,

and the morally unthinkable becomes the thinkable as the years move on.[2]

Schaeffer, writing in the 1970s, perceptively continued,

> The thinkables of the eighties and nineties will certainly include things which most people today find unthinkable and immoral, even unimaginable and too extreme to suggest. Yet—since they do not have some overriding principle that takes them beyond relativistic thinking—when these become thinkable and acceptable in the eighties and nineties, most people will not even remember that they were unthinkable in the seventies. They will slide into each new thinkable without a jolt.[3]

Schaeffer was not arguing that something is worthy of emulation simply because it was previously done. By itself, Dad and Mom's conduct, while often qualitatively better and more polite than that of their children observed at the local mall, is not an adequate standard for morality. In fact, the point is that the basis of yesterday's morality was of such poor quality that it could not prevent its "unthinkables" from becoming "thinkables" in short order. One of yesterday's unthinkables—the social and moral acceptance of homosexuality in both orientation and act, in both desire and deed—is presented to us today as quite thinkable, and though we are speaking of morality and not the changing tides of fashion, our modern society can seldom tell the difference.

Furthermore, we must recognize with Schaeffer that this is the way things play out when performed upon a *humanistic* stage that views man (or, more precisely, self) as the lead character—the measure of all things, the center of it all—and casts God (if He even exists) in a subordinate role. In much of this discussion, God has been relegated to the periphery and man has taken His place. This practice is reflected in the quip "God created man in His image, and ever since man has returned the favor." A humanistic approach to morality suffers from the "immaculate perception" that says, "My ways are always right and everything else must fit." This approach has the effect (whether admitted or not) of viewing God's standards of morality to be the equivalent of a wax nose—capable of being shaped according to the whim of the shaper. "Wax nose" morality renders God's moral pronouncements to be temporary and optional. In all of this, God's authority is questioned ("Has God said?"[4]), and therefore, what God has declared about righteous behavior may make for nice history (for other people!) and perhaps exhibit keen insights from which we may glean some guidance, but is, according to this new (im-)morality, archaic and repressive. We are witnessing what happens when God's absolute, authoritative standard is removed or redefined. Sliding into some kind of "new morality," some kind of the unthinkable, and doing it without a jolt becomes easy.

HOMOSEXUALITY ... CONSISTENT WITH THE BIBLE?

As noted above, however, this clamor for the acceptability of homosexuality, which is heard even in the church, is not without a *stated* authoritative base. The people making this claim appeal to the Bible and assert that a homosexual lifestyle is perfectly compatible with its teaching.

The same-sex controversy is, at its core, a controversy over the authority and interpretation of the Bible. Throughout the history of the church, and revealed in the historical understanding of Scripture,[5] homosexuality has been seen as contrary to the morality set forth in the pages of the Bible. Today, however, we are being told that the moral opposition to homosexuality, based in and upon Scripture, is actually a rather recent phenomenon. We are being "informed" that the Bible nowhere condemns homosexuality as it is predominantly known and practiced today and that, as a matter of fact, a lifestyle of committed homosexuality is consistent with biblical morality.

Ironically, this makes for a remarkable case of selectivity in submitting to biblical authority. What we are observing is, on one hand, a mocking rejection of much of the teaching of the Older Testament and, on the other hand, a claim that the Bible endorses homosexuality. It is not uncommon to hear ridiculing murmurs about many things in the Bible, including the authority and observance of the Sabbath, dietary and cleanliness (or purification) laws, legislation regarding slavery, the death penalty, the sacrificial system, and the priesthood, just to name a few. Yet these criticisms are uttered with the same breath that exclaims with incredulity, "Why do you quote the Bible regarding homosexuality but ignore these other matters?"

While suspicious of the Older Testament's laws and practices, the proponents of the acceptability of homosexuality in the church will wax on with great deference and approval about the passages that speak of close personal relationships between members of the same sex (Jonathan and David or Ruth and Naomi, for example).[6] They claim these as examples of beautiful homosexual relationships worthy of emulation. Supposedly, we are not to follow the Bible in some areas (deemed irrelevant or inconvenient), but we are to follow its lead in other places. Selectivity indeed.

This claim of biblical support for a homosexual lifestyle is surprising to many. After all, is not the Bible clear in its prohibition of homosexuality? Historically, has not the church consistently rejected homosexuality since it is out of accord with biblical morality? What about all of the passages that . . . well . . . so clearly condemn homosexuality? What about these? Have they been misunderstood and misinterpreted and misapplied for all these years? One thinks of God's institution of marriage—it is to be between one man and one woman. How does the current agenda challenge this design? What of the account of the destruction of the city of Sodom or the clear prohibitions of homosexuality that one finds in the book of Leviticus? What of the apostle Paul's writing on the subject in Romans, 1 Corinthians, and 1 Timothy? Has there been any question that Paul considered homosexual longing or behavior to be inconsistent with a God-pleasing life?

Those advocating the compatibility of homosexuality

with the Bible appeal, of necessity, to these very passages, for they claim that the Bible *does not* condemn but *does* condone such a practice. More and more the Bible is seen to somehow fall in line with modern "science" and modern impulses. Wherever the Bible opposes homosexuality, these passages are reinterpreted and re-presented so that the modern reader can now "understand" the original context, which was apparently hidden, lost, or buried under a load of cultural bias. The net effect of this revisionist approach is a novel and destructive twisting of Scripture: each passage is considered and, lo and behold, we find that same-sex intimacy is not even being considered, or that the passage addresses an *abuse* of the supposedly proper place of same-sex intimacy.

The Authority of the Bible

In past decades homosexuals were ashamed to "go public." Historically, theologians were not required to address this topic, as it was commonly understood to be a violation of God's law. Francis Turretin, a theologian of the seventeenth century, simply referred to homosexuality as "the sin against nature."[7] Previously, homosexuals rarely tried to go to the Bible to obtain approval for their behavior and appetites—they knew it was not to be found. Lately, since public opinion has turned slightly in their favor, the shame has diminished to the point where the Bible is being pursued as an ally, as a moral reference point to bolster their position. After all, if the Bible can be summoned to the homosexuals' defense, they may have a case.

So in the midst of this present debate, adherents to both sides of the same-sex controversy claim the authority of the Bible in their defense. Both sides claim that the Bible is clear. Both sides claim to have moral justification for their position. However, both sides cannot be correct. If God's Word prohibits something, the church must prohibit it as well. The church must not remain silent where God's Word speaks.

The Bible speaks of its own authority. It must. As God's Word, it cannot speak, or admit, of any higher authority; to do so would be to present itself as a lesser authority. For our purposes, understanding the Bible's own pronouncements regarding its authority is important for at least two reasons.

First, the question of the moral acceptability of homosexuality cannot be answered solely by the individual texts that specifically speak of homosexuality; the entire teaching of Scripture—especially its teaching on marriage—is relevant to our discussion. As we consider what the Bible has to say about marriage (in chapter 8), we will see that a biblical definition of marriage leaves no room for homosexual intimacy or homosexual marriage.

Second, if the authority of the Bible, the *stated* consensus of those on both sides of this issue, is to be maintained, we will see that the Bible cannot truly be shown to approve of homosexual practice or desire. Even from the passages that are often cited by advocates of the acceptability of homosexuality within the Christian faith, the Bible from cover to cover, in passage after passage, disapproves of homosexuality, calling it sin yet offering hope for those who are struggling with it.

The interpretive approach of those who advocate the acceptability of homosexuality from the teaching of the Bible challenge the authority of Scripture at every point and on each passage. These revisionists point to the Law of God as found in Leviticus and say that these passages do not apply to the modern day. While speaking of allegiance to the Bible, they revise the clear teaching of the Bible with regard to homosexuality. The psalmist, however, thought otherwise: "Thy righteousness is an *everlasting* righteousness, and Thy Law is truth" (119:142). Yet the Bible says that the "Scripture *cannot* be broken" (John 10:35) and "all [God's] precepts are sure. They are upheld *forever and ever*, they are performed in truth and uprightness" (Psalm 111:7–8) (emphasis added).

In Conclusion

We must view the present-day controversy over homosexuality as evidence that some have rejected the authority of the Word of God: even some in the church. It is possible for the "law to be lost" among those who claim to be followers of God, and there is indeed a "famine in the land . . . a famine for hearing the words of the LORD" (see Ezekiel 7:26 and Amos 8:11–12). Many in the contemporary church have been drinking from the well of relativism rather than consuming the absolute truth of God's Word. This is precisely what society at large has done in previous generations; they have denied the existence of that which is absolute, invariant, and universal. They have denied God's Word, and, as a result, call that which is evil good and good evil. This error has crept into the church, and she has embraced this re-tooled idol (Ezekiel 33:17–20). In truth, Christianity stands against relativism. Christianity is grounded upon the basis of antithesis: God is distinct from His creation and has declared that which is good and that which is evil. He has interpreted all of existence, including marriage and the relations allowed within marriage. Whenever we deny God's interpretation of reality, whenever we reject His determination of righteousness and unrighteousness, we drift in the morass of relativism, having denied the existence of absolutes. This is what Francis Schaeffer referred to as "philosophic homosexuality." Schaeffer wrote,

> Some forms of homosexuality are of a similar nature, in that they are not just homosexuality but a philosophic problem. One must have understanding for the real homophile's problem. But much modern homosexuality is an expression of the current denial of antithesis. It has led in this case to an obliteration of the distinction between man and woman. So the male and the female as complementary partners are finished.... In much modern thinking, all antithesis and all of the order of God's creation is to be fought against—including the male-female distinctions. The pressure toward uni-sex is

largely rooted here. But this is not an isolated problem; it is a part of the world-spirit of the generation that surrounds us. It is imperative that Christians realize the conclusions that are being drawn as a result of the death of absolutes.[8]

Why This Book?

This revisionist approach is at the heart of the current controversy. The Bible is being reinterpreted according to urges that are "against nature" and then said to support the homosexual agenda. We believe that such claims are entirely false and must be answered. We will examine each of the passages to which homosexuality advocates appeal and show the incompatibility of homosexuality and biblical Christianity. We will do this by considering the revisionist approaches to these passages and show the historical understandings to be correct. In our view, doing so will expose these modern revisions as utterly insufficient and reveal the absence of any authoritative foundation upon which such claims are made. Despite the revisionists' protests to the contrary, their position is in actuality based upon human desire rather than upon biblical authority and interpretation.

It is our hope that this book will prove helpful to those who are confused by this controversy—whether they are struggling with homosexual sin, know of someone who is, or just want to properly understand what the Bible actually teaches. We have endeavored to design this book so that the reader may easily find information on a particular biblical text that is being cited by those who claim biblical support for homosexuality.

Responsibility and Response

George Grant and Mark Horne have said,

> It is the sad tendency of modern men to either do the right thing in the wrong way or to do the wrong thing in the right way. We either hold to the truth obnoxiously or we hold to a lie graciously. We are either a rude angel or a polite devil. Often what poses as a cruel orthodoxy is defeated by what poses as a kind heresy.[9]

The authors of this book are ordained ministers of the gospel and, as such, have a responsibility to shepherd the flock of God, which is the church. We have a responsibility to "hold fast the faithful word which is in accordance with the teaching" so as "to exhort in sound doctrine and to refute those who contradict" (Titus 1:9). While it is possible that some may view this book as inflammatory, unloving, or even unchristian, the opposite is actually the case. In accordance with Titus 1:9, exhortation with the truth (sound doctrine) and the refutation of that which is false is a nonnegotiable duty for the Christian minister. Christian ministers must instruct *and* refute. Some ideas are bad and wrong—these must be exposed for the health of the church and the honor of Jesus Christ. Beware of false accusations on both sides of this controversy. The authors do not believe that every homosexual is a child molester or that homosexuality is the unpardonable sin. Conversely, it must be acknowledged that our disagreement with homosexuality—in proclivity or in practice—as consistent with biblical morality does not render us hateful. The authors of this book are not homophobic, legalistic, or sinfully judgmental, and the true definitions of these terms are often ignored when they are applied to those who disagree with the homosexuality advocates' view.

Having stated our position, we do not contend that Christian ministers are permitted to perform their duties in a cement-headed and heavy-handed way. On the contrary, Christian ministers, if they are to be faithful shepherds, must present the truth in a truthful way. We must be Christian in our doctrine and in our duty. Presenting the truth in this way is an expression of faithfulness to God and God's people, and is, therefore, loving. We, therefore, submit this book for the glory of God and the strengthening of His church.

Notes

1. Some will assert that the Bible knows and teaches nothing of an *orientation* (inclination, proclivity) toward homosexuality as a lifestyle and that the Bible only condemns homosexual behavior or deeds. This view will be shown to be false. The Bible condemns both the practice of an evil deed and the inclination toward an evil deed. Homosexuality, either as an interest in intimacy (inclination) or as an intimate interest (behavior) in a person of the same sex is forbidden. Both the desire and the deed are considered immoral in the Bible.

2. C. Everett Koop and Francis Schaeffer, *Whatever Happened to the Human Race?*, revised edition (Wheaton, Ill.: Crossway Books, 1983), 2.

3. Ibid., 3.

4. Genesis 3:1.

5. See chapter 8 of this book.

6. See Tom Horner, *Jonathan Loved David: Homosexuality in Biblical Times* (Philadelphia: Westminster Press, 1978), chapters 2–3.

7. Francis Turretin, *Institutes of Elenctic Theology*, trans. George Musgrave Cider; James T. Dennison, ed. (Phillipsburg, N.J.: Presbyterian and Reformed, 1994). Turretin's words could be applied to our own day without any doubt. While demonstrating various forms of illicit intercourse to be examples of adultery (violations of the Seventh Commandment), he included homosexuality and bestiality as examples. He wrote that such violations comprise "the sin against nature and those horrible crimes expressed by the words *sodomy* and *bestiality* (of which mention is made in Leviticus 20:13 and Romans 1:27, which are not even to be named among Christians, although even now

they prevail too much in various places to the disgrace of the Christian name)" (vol. 2, 121).

8. Francis Schaeffer, *The God Who Is There*. The Complete Works of Francis Schaeffer, Vol. 1 (Wheaton, Ill.: Crossway Books, 1982), 37.

9. George Grant and Mark Horne, *Unnatural Affections: The Impuritan Ethic of Homosexuality and the Modern Church* (Nashville: Legacy Press, 1991), 70.

CHAPTER TWO

Revisiting Sodom:
The Lesson of Sodom and Gomorrah

The manner in which man is to live as the creation of God, made in His image, is so fundamental, so basic that one of the earliest narratives in Scripture reflects clearly upon the wickedness involved in the violation of God's purposes for mankind. We are hardly overstating the case to say that the story of Sodom and Gomorrah has, as long as the collective memory of the Jewish and Christian people can be determined, been understood to speak directly to the issue of homosexuality. The constant drumbeat of pro-homosexual explanations of this passage, however, seems intent on drowning out its plain meaning as well as the historical consistency of how it has been understood since it was written under the direction of God's Spirit. But before the revisionist views of Sodom and Gomorrah can be addressed, we must consider the passage in its own context and revisit this startling example of God's judgment.

SODOM AND GOMORRAH: ORIGINAL CONTEXT

As in any good narrative, the Scriptures indicate that not all was going to go well with Lot. In Genesis 13, Abram and Lot develop a problem of being overly blessed with livestock and possessions. Wisdom demands that they part company, and Lot looks toward the Jordan River valley and decides the grass looks greener in that direction. After Scripture records Lot's decision, a short, easily overlooked comment is made. Genesis 13:13 reads, "Now the men of Sodom were wicked exceedingly and sinners against the LORD." No further expansion is offered. Just a simple statement that the *men* of Sodom were exceedingly wicked. They were rebels against God. We simply note in passing that the writer elsewhere used the more generic term "people" when referring to groups of people (Genesis 11:6; 14:16, 21), but here he specifically focuses upon the *men* of Sodom, not just the *people* of Sodom. Further, their sinfulness long preceded any of the events recorded in chapters 18 and 19. This becomes significant when examining revisionist attempts to redefine the thrust of the story.

Some time later the events of Genesis 18 and 19

unfold. Abram is visited by three "men." We are told that this group is actually made up of two angels and the Lord himself (Genesis 18:22; 19:1). After showing hospitality to these visitors, Abram accompanies them toward Sodom and Gomorrah. In Genesis 18, the Lord reveals that He is about to bring judgment upon these cities:

> 20And the LORD said, "The outcry of Sodom and Gomorrah is indeed great, and their sin is exceedingly grave. 21I will go down now, and see if they have done entirely according to its outcry, which has come to Me; and if not, I will know."

For the second time the text speaks of the greatness of the sin of Sodom and Gomorrah. So strong is the description of the rebellion of these cities that God sends the angels to the cities for direct contact with these rebel sinners. Abram, realizing Lot is among these men, seeks to save the cities if as few as ten righteous men can be found within them. This provides the background for the key passage, found in the first section of Genesis 19.

> 1Now the two angels came to Sodom in the evening as Lot was sitting in the gate of Sodom. When Lot saw them, he rose to meet them and bowed down with his face to the ground. 2And he said, "Now behold, my lords, please turn aside into your servant's house, and spend the night, and wash your feet; then you may rise early and go on your way." They said however, "No, but we shall spend the night in the square." 3Yet he urged them strongly, so they turned aside to him and entered

his house; and he prepared a feast for them, and baked unleavened bread, and they ate.

Lot sits in the city gate as evening falls in Sodom. As he had come into the area a wealthy man, with flocks and herds, he would have been in the upper echelon of society. To sit in the city gate was a position of honor.

Lot immediately recognizes these strangers are not ordinary travelers. Just as Abram had recognized their special nature, Lot too responds with unusual concern. Ancient societies required the extension of hospitality to traveling strangers, especially due to the rather obvious fact that the land was yet wild, cities and towns were few and far between, and therefore the giving of aid and shelter was vitally important. But we see immediately that Lot goes beyond the norm, for after offering food and shelter, he says, "Then you may rise early and go on your way." Lot wants these men to get *out* of Sodom as quickly as possible. Why? Lot knew the character of the city, and seemingly he sensed the character of these men as well. He knew they were in danger in this place.

The angels, however, know more than Lot does. They press the issue, testing him, saying they will stay the night out in the open city square. Surely there is no more exposed place in all of Sodom than the city square, the hub of civic life, and Lot "urged them strongly," pleading with them not to follow this course but to come with him to his house. The angels are persuaded and accompany Lot. A feast follows, as Lot surely has the wherewithal to provide for the strangers.

Immediately it should be noted that Lot's actions indicate his fears for the safety of these travelers. He is not afraid that they will simply be ignored in the city square. His actions are not those of a man worried that they will not get a hot meal or an invitation to spend the night in a home if they should continue inside and enter the city square. There is something far more than inhospitality in view here.

> [4]Before they lay down, the men of the city, the men
> of Sodom, surrounded the house, both young and old,
> all the people from every quarter . . .

The night is not far spent when the situation worsens. The feast over, Lot realizes his intentions have become known to the men of the city. Surely, despite his best efforts, the visitors had been seen. Word has spread, and the house is now surrounded.

We must note that the text takes pains to inform us that this is not a small group representing only a fraction of the city's population. This is not a minority group. Notice two things: first, the crowd is made up of men, and men only. By repeating itself, the text makes sure we realize these are men who are surrounding Lot's home. It says, "the men of the city, the men of Sodom." Second, it tells us that the entire city, young and old, and every quarter, rich or poor, is represented in the gathered crowd. And they are not merely at the front door. They surround the house, so great is the crowd.

Lot does not immediately open the door. But they

soon make their presence and intentions known.

> [5]. . . and they called to Lot and said to him, "Where are the men who came to you tonight? Bring them out to us that we may have relations with them."

The crowd knows Lot has received visitors—male visitors, specifically. The crowd instructs Lot to bring out these men so "that we may have relations with them." As this phrase is probably the most controversial element of the entire story, we need to consider well what is being said. The NASB renders the phrase "have relations with them." The NIV says, "so that we can have sex with them." The NKJV expresses it, "that we may know them *carnally.*" Each of these translations is rendering the basic phrase "that we may know them." The key issue has to do with the meaning of the word *know.* Does it mean "know them" as in get acquainted with, exchange business cards and e-mail addresses? Or, as the NASB, NIV, and NKJV indicate, does it have a sexual overtone?

The Hebrew term used by the writer is *yada.* Its general meaning is *to know.* In the majority of its uses in the Old Testament, it carries that basic meaning, that of knowing something or someone. So why would major translations render it in a sexual manner?

The answer is both contextual and linguistic. The context bears this meaning with clarity. Further, the term *is* used of "knowing" someone sexually. When Adam "knew" Eve she had a child as a result (Genesis 4:1, 17, 25). This usage occurs in the same book as the story of

Sodom. The translators of the Septuagint, the Greek version of the Old Testament, likewise understood *yada* in this way, using a Greek term that has the specific meaning of "sexual intercourse."[1]

But the context becomes the key, as we see in the following few verses.

> [6]But Lot went out to them at the doorway, and shut the door behind him, [7]and said, "Please, my brothers, do not act wickedly.
>
> [8]"Now behold, I have two daughters who have not had relations with man; please let me bring them out to you, and do to them whatever you like; only do nothing to these men, inasmuch as they have come under the shelter of my roof."

Again we note that, in some sense, Lot expected this. His fear of allowing the strangers to stay in the city square has come to fruition: he knew the men of Sodom would act in just this fashion. He goes out to them, seeking to attempt to reason with them, but he makes sure to shut the door, too. He does not introduce the visitors, but keeps them in the relative safety of his home.

Lot addresses these men of Sodom as "brothers," for he sat in the city gate and hopes that his presence among them will give him some standing, some chance of changing their minds. Yet, we see also again that these are the *men* of Sodom, not a mixed group of men and women, for he speaks only of "brothers."

But in the very same sentence Lot speaks the words

that enrage the crowd. To this point we only have the crowd desiring that the strangers be brought out to them. But when Lot identifies their *desire* as "wicked," he surely violates their sense of "political correctness" and angers them. Clearly Lot knows what the crowd meant by "know them," and he identifies the desire on the part of these men for sexual contact with the male visitors as "wickedness." It is surely no mere coincidence that the writer uses the same word for "wicked" here that he used in Genesis 13:13 when the sinfulness of Sodom was first introduced. There cannot be any doubt that the sinfulness known in Genesis 13, the wickedness of which God speaks in Genesis 18:20, is here seen in its full expression in the lustful, homosexual desire of the men of Sodom for these visitors.

At this point we encounter the sad, strange offer of Lot regarding his virgin daughters. Before considering how Lot could make such an offer, it should be noted that this verse establishes, beyond all reasonable doubt, the essential correctness of the translation of *yada* given in the NASB and NIV at verse 5, that of a desire for *sexual* contact with the visitors. Lot's daughters, he says, have not "known" man, that is, they are virgins. The same Hebrew word, *yada,* is used here as in verse 5. Obviously, it has the same meaning in both passages: sexual activity, sexual "knowledge." Lot has not misunderstood the desire of the men of Sodom. He is not so out of touch with reality that upon hearing these men just want to "welcome" the visitors to the city that he offers his daughters to them so that they can do with them whatever they want! The context, then, is plain in its meaning.

Yet we still have to ask, how could any father make such an offer? Surely we can say with confidence that the angels would never have allowed this to take place, had the men even accepted the offer. But are we forced to simply condemn Lot as an unloving man who was willing to offer his daughters to be ravished by a crowd of men?

One alternative possibility does exist. Lot knew these men. He knew their lifestyle, their activities. Seemingly a sort of truce existed between him and the homosexual inhabitants of Sodom: they did not seek to involve him in their activities, and he did not speak out against them. It is possible that Lot is simply buying time, knowing that, in fact, the offer will not be accepted, for these men simply do not have any desire for women. He may feel his daughters are perfectly safe, for those standing before him had shown a firm and unwavering desire for sexual fulfillment with men, not with women.

Yet even here Lot has already crossed the line in his description of their desire as "wicked." While he pleads that he cannot allow anything to happen to these men, as they are under his protection (another ancient element to the story, drawing on the requirement of giving aid and protection to any visitor under your roof, which would be all the more the requirement for members of his own household), he has closed their ears through his implicit condemnation of their very desire *to* be so engaged with the strangers. His offer is not taken seriously, and the crowd is quickly enraged. They have made their intentions known: anyone who would stand in their way, especially for *moral* reasons, is an insult and offense to them.

> [9]But they said, "Stand aside." Furthermore, they said, "This one came in as an alien, and already he is acting like a judge; now we will treat you worse than them." So they pressed hard against Lot and came near to break the door.

The first response from the gathered crowd of men is to simply ignore Lot's response. "Stand aside!" they command. If he will not cooperate with their desires, they will take matters into their own hands. But others focus upon Lot, recognizing that he is not a native Sodomite. "How dare he judge *us!*" is their cry. Lot dared to identify their desires for the strangers as wicked. How dare he force his morality upon them! And so they come at Lot, who vainly attempts to hold off the crowd. Backed to the door, Lot is in desperate straits.

> [10]But the men reached out their hands and brought Lot into the house with them, and shut the door. [11]And they struck the men who were at the doorway of the house with blindness, both small and great, so that they wearied themselves trying to find the doorway.

Moral blindness precedes physical blindness. The now angry mob at the front door, unaware of the actual nature of the men inside the house and their impending doom, continues to press their passions. The angels retrieve Lot, seemingly with supernatural power, and shut the door tightly. They then strike the men seeking to enter the house with blindness. Their action is both preventive (instant blindness will surely be an impediment to getting the door open) as well as extensive: all of them, both small and great, are struck blind.

One of the most striking statements in the entire narrative, however, follows immediately after the action of the angels in blinding the men: "They wearied themselves trying to find the doorway." What an utterly amazing commentary on the power of man's lust and anger at having his sin exposed and judged wicked. Any rational man, upon losing his sight while attempting to do what is so obviously sinful and evil, would at least *hesitate* and ponder the meaning of this sudden event. And when it became obvious that everyone else had likewise been blinded, what other possible conclusion could be reached than, "What we are doing is wrong; we had better cease and desist immediately." Yet these are men whose wickedness is so great, who have been so given over to their lusts, that such thoughts do not deter them. They weary themselves in their pursuit of their goal, but they are supernaturally kept from obtaining it.

We should note that though these men did not actually *accomplish* their desires, they are still identified as wicked. The distinction between act and desire that is so often a part of modern discussions is not to be found in the ancient text.

The angels have accomplished their mission. The

report concerning Sodom has surely been shown to be true. The "outcry" that has come to God matches the reality completely. Sodom will now become a byword for sinfulness and debauchery, but first, mercy is expressed to Lot and his family.

> [12]Then the [two] men said to Lot, "Whom else have you here? A son-in-law, and your sons, and your daughters, and whomever you have in the city, bring them out of the place; [13]for we are about to destroy this place, because their outcry has become so great before the LORD that the LORD has sent us to destroy it."

There is clear urgency in the angels' words. They have been sent to destroy this place, a judgment upon the wickedness of the men who are even then exhausting themselves outside the door trying to find a way in so as to gratify their homosexual lusts with the strangers. Lot tries to comply with the angels' exhortation.

> [14]Lot went out and spoke to his sons-in-law, who were to marry his daughters, and said, "Up, get out of this place, for the LORD will destroy the city." But he appeared to his sons-in-law to be jesting.

What an incredible experience it must have been to leave the house in the darkness, still surrounded by the enraged and blinded crowd. Lot could not have been overly collected when he located his prospective sons-in-law, but despite this, they show no respect for him or for his warning. Lot surely knew, as he returned to his home, that he had made the wrong decision that day when Abraham had offered him whatever part of the land he desired. He knew of Sodom's reputation, but had gone that direction anyway. Now he was paying the price. He knew these prospective sons-in-law were not godly men and would not be husbands who would follow the ways of the Lord. Now they would be swept away with the rest of the city's residents, despite their knowledge of the coming judgment.

> 15When morning dawned, the angels urged Lot, saying, "Up, take your wife and your two daughters, who are here, lest you be swept away in the punishment of the city."
> 16But he hesitated. So the men seized his hand and the hand of his wife and the hands of his two daughters, for the compassion of the LORD was upon him; and they brought him out, and put him outside the city.

Time was running out. Judgment was swiftly approaching, and in their mercy, the angels urged Lot to take the few he had with him and flee to safety. But amazingly, despite all he had seen, despite the events of the evening, despite his knowing the coming judgment was utterly just and righteous, he hesitates. Was it his possessions that kept his heart there? We are not told. But God's compassion was upon him, so the angels once again demonstrate that no man is a match for their strength, and they simply grab Lot, his wife, and his daughters, and bring them out of the city.

The rest of the story is well known. God's judgment falls swiftly upon Sodom and Gomorrah, and the destruction is complete. None escape, and even Lot's wife, who perhaps cannot separate herself from the worldly possessions that held her heart captive, is struck down because of her refusal, in the face of God's mercy, to remain obedient. The smoke from the destruction climbs high into the sky, and Abraham himself sees the sure sign that God did not, in fact, find even ten righteous in the city of Sodom.

Objections Considered

Through the centuries the story of Sodom and Gomorrah has been understood to communicate God's wrath against sin, and in particular, against the sin of homosexuality. But in recent decades revisionist authors have launched a full-scale assault upon the passage, seeking to render it irrelevant to the topic of homosexuality. A number of different (and often contradictory) arguments have been brought forward, the collective force of which has been to remove this incident from the biblical data upon which a decision concerning the sinfulness of homosexuality should be based.[2]

We will consider first the only meaningful argument, biblically speaking, then we will move to other, more creative arguments.

Objection Stated

> *The rest of Scripture, Old and New Testament, does not identify the sin of Sodom as homosexuality, but instead speaks of inhospitality, mistreatment of the poor, and other general sins of behavior as the basis of God's judgment. This silence regarding homosexuality proves that the traditional reading is in error.*

Daniel Helminiak, a Roman Catholic priest, is representative of this argument when he says,

> But in this particular case the meaning of the text is obvious from other parts of the Bible. For the Bible often refers back to the story of Sodom and says outright what Sodom's sin was.
>
> The prophet Ezekiel (16:48–49) states the case boldly: "This was the guilt of your sister Sodom: she and her daughters had pride, surfeit of food and prosperous ease, but did not aid the poor and needy." The sin of the Sodomites was that they refused to take in the needy travelers.[3]

Biblical Response

Is this the conclusion one must draw from an examination of this and other passages in the Bible concerning Sodom and Gomorrah? Surely not. In the above citation, Helminiak stops too early. Note the full passage:

> [48]"As I live," declares the LORD God, "Sodom, your sister, and her daughters have not done as you and your

daughters have done. [49]Behold, this was the guilt of your sister Sodom: she and her daughters had arrogance, abundant food, and careless ease, but she did not help the poor and needy. [50]Thus they were haughty and committed abominations before Me. Therefore I removed them when I saw it."

The citation of verse 50 completely changes the conclusions we must reach by listening to the text.[4] There is surely no question that the appearance of the term *abominations*, and how it is obviously differentiated from the inhospitality and heartlessness of the inhabitants of Sodom and Gomorrah (and in fact is seen as the *result* of their indolence and pride), takes us directly back to the issues so clearly laid out in Genesis 19. The judgment of God is directly linked to the commission of *abominations*, the Hebrew word associated with homosexuality in His law (Leviticus 18:22; 20:13).

It is not denied that the inhabitants of Sodom were an inhospitable people, but it must be remembered that sin is rarely "alone" in the lives of those who revel in it. Sin is often a complex of attitudes and actions, joined together by a common thread of rebellion against God and His ways. Indeed, arrogance and pride are closely related to a willingness to twist even the most basic and fundamental aspect of our being, our sexuality, and to flaunt this in the face of God and our fellow creatures. So to point to *other* sins of Sodom and Gomorrah as if this means homosexuality was *not* part and parcel of the sin of the cities is to assume far too narrow a range of sin in their experience.

Sodom and Gomorrah is so closely linked with God's wrath, giving, as it does, one of the earliest examples of the pouring out of His wrath in the period after the Flood, that it became a byword for sinfulness that brings certain judgment.[5] It likewise is referenced as evidence of the hardheartedness of sinners who simply refuse to repent in the face of certain doom. Jeremiah 23:14 speaks of those who refuse to turn back from their wickedness as being like Sodom.

Objection Stated

It is highly unlikely that "know" in Genesis 19 means to know sexually or in a homosexual context. The word is used over nine hundred times in the Bible, and it simply does not refer to homosexual activity in any of those instances.

Biblical Response

It is surely true that *yada* does not refer to sexual activity in the majority of its appearances. Given that the word means *both* to "know" in the sense of knowing factual information *and* to "know" intimately in a sexual fashion, one would hardly expect that the discussion of sexual activity would predominate over the discussion of knowing facts, people, or events. Of course the majority of references will be to the more normative use. But does it follow that the term cannot be defined contextually, as it is in Genesis 19? Surely not.

In addition, aside from the clear contextual indication of homosexuality in Genesis 19, such an objection overlooks the situation in Judges 19, which provides a very close parallel to the Sodom story. And while many revisionists dismiss this passage on the same basis as they do the Sodom incident, Judges 19:22–25 only proves the correctness of the interpretation of Sodom and Gomorrah already offered. Note the text of Judges 19:22–25:

> [22]While they were making merry, behold, the men of the city, certain worthless fellows, surrounded the house, pounding the door; and they spoke to the owner of the house, the old man, saying, "Bring out the man who came into your house that we may have relations with him."
>
> [23]Then the man, the owner of the house, went out to them and said to them, "No, my fellows, please do not act so wickedly; since this man has come into my house, do not commit this act of folly. [24]Here is my virgin daughter and his concubine. Please let me bring them out that you may ravish them and do to them whatever you wish. But do not commit such an act of folly against this man."
>
> [25]But the men would not listen to him. So the man seized his concubine and brought her out to them; and they raped her and abused her all night until morning, then let her go at the approach of dawn.

The Hebrew word *yada* is used in verse 22, "that we may have relations with him." Does this merely mean "get to know"? Surely not. In the context this man had sat out in the city square, no one caring about him. Any hospitable person would have had all the opportunity in the world to "get to know" him in that way. No, as the response of the householder shows, theirs was a wicked desire. But just as in Genesis 19, the rest of the story clinches the debate. The very same word is used in verse 25: "and they raped her," literally, "they *knew* her." *Yada* here is obviously sexual, hence, the use in verse 22 would be in reference to homosexual "knowing."

Objection Stated

Jesus mentioned Sodom and Gomorrah, but never connected the Sodom story with anything relevant to homosexuality. Instead, He connected Sodom and Gomorrah to inhospitality, proving that the traditional interpretation of the passage is in error.

Biblical Response

Matthew 10:14–15 records the words of the Lord,

Whoever does not receive you, nor heed your words, as you go out of that house or that city, shake the dust off your feet. Truly I say to you, it will be more tolerable for the land of Sodom and Gomorrah in the day of judgment, than for that city.

While it is admitted that Jesus does not speak of homosexuality in connection with the destruction of Sodom and

Gomorrah, it must also be admitted that Jesus nowhere refers to their sin as that of inhospitality. It is inappropriate to assume that Jesus is approving of the revisionist interpretation of the Genesis account of the destruction of Sodom as due *solely* to inhospitality. This assumption is made because the judgment of Sodom is placed in the context of people not receiving the disciples. Such an interpretation completely ignores the fact that Sodom's judgment had become axiomatic for the fullest outpouring of God's wrath throughout the Old Testament. It is not a matter of the cities of Jesus' day being *inhospitable* to the disciples, as if they would not provide food, water, or shelter. Instead, these cities refused to hear the good news of the gospel. Theirs was a hardhearted rejection, just as was seen in Jeremiah 23:14, for which they would suffer swift retribution.

The error of the revisionist is in thinking that Jesus is here even raising the *nature* of the original sin of Sodom and Gomorrah. The issue is that these cities will be held accountable to God for their grievous sins. And the comparison is that it will be more tolerable for Sodom and Gomorrah in that day than for those cities that had experienced the visitation of the very apostles of the incarnate Lord, but refused their message of repentance and faith. While Sodom and Gomorrah received only the witness of one man's inconsistent life (Lot), these cities were guilty of shutting their eyes to the glaring brightness of the light of the gospel itself, brought to them by the Lord's disciples. This is what prompts the words of the Lord.

Objection Stated

The references to Sodom in Jude and 2 Peter do not condemn homosexuality. Jude speaks of desiring "strange flesh," and Peter refers only to sexual immorality, not to homosexuality. Some assert that the sin of the Sodomites in Jude consisted of a desire to have sexual relations with angels. Both passages show us that the attempt to connect the Genesis story with homosexuality lacks the support of New Testament writers.

Biblical Response

The two passages under consideration are Jude 6–7 and 2 Peter 2:4–10. Jude writes,

> ⁶And angels who did not keep their own domain, but abandoned their proper abode, He has kept in eternal bonds under darkness for the judgment of the great day. ⁷Just as Sodom and Gomorrah and the cities around them, since they in the same way as these indulged in gross immorality and went after strange flesh, are exhibited as an example in undergoing the punishment of eternal fire.

And Peter addresses the same issue by writing,

> ⁴For if God did not spare angels when they sinned, but cast them into hell and committed them to pits of darkness, reserved for judgment, ⁵and did not spare the ancient world, but preserved Noah, a preacher of

righteousness, with seven others, when He brought a flood upon the world of the ungodly; [6]and if He condemned the cities of Sodom and Gomorrah to destruction by reducing them to ashes, having made them an example to those who would live ungodly lives thereafter; [7]and if He rescued righteous Lot, oppressed by the sensual conduct of unprincipled men [8](for by what he saw and heard that righteous man, while living among them, felt his righteous soul tormented day after day by their lawless deeds), [9]then the Lord knows how to rescue the godly from temptation, and to keep the unrighteous under punishment for the day of judgment, [10]and especially those who indulge the flesh in its corrupt desires and despise authority.

Both passages follow directly in line with the use of Sodom and Gomorrah as the icon for sexual debauchery and unrepentant evil. Jude describes Sodom and Gomorrah as a symbol, a type, an example of God's punishment upon gross immorality. Jude makes a direct connection between the judgment upon angels who "abandoned their proper abode" and the inhabitants of Sodom and Gomorrah who "indulged in gross immorality and went after strange flesh." Surely these are not words that can be made to describe mere inhospitality! Some have attempted to avoid the weight of the description of going after "strange flesh" by saying that the sin here is that the men desired to engage in relations with angels. While this would surely amount to going after "strange flesh," there is one rather obvious problem with this idea. *The men of*

Sodom did not know the visitors were angels. They believed them to be mere men, like themselves.

Therefore, Jude's description is best understood to refer to the homosexual desire of the men to engage in relations with the visitors. Here the Scriptures use very strong language to describe homosexual desire. The first term is a strengthened form of the standard word for sexual immorality and debauchery. The second term, rendered "strange flesh" by the NASB but more interpretively as "pursued unnatural lust" in the NRSV and "perversion" in the NIV, literally means "flesh of a different kind."

How should this be understood? Given the background, this would surely be in reference to homosexuality. Why, since homosexuality is a desire for flesh *of the same kind?* Because the natural desire of man is for the woman, not for man. The "unnatural lust" or "perversion" here referred to is that which causes a man to lust for *different* flesh than that which God intended. Just as the angels did not remain in the place where God intended (verse 6), but abandoned their created purpose, so these men abandoned what was natural and pursued what was unnatural: homosexuality.

Peter's description parallels this, describing the regular activities of the inhabitants of Sodom and Gomorrah as *daily* being ungodly and wicked. Peter speaks of the "filthy lives of lawless men" (NIV), the "licentiousness of the lawless" (NRSV), or the "filthy conduct of the wicked" (NKJV). Clearly Peter likewise interpreted the sinful acts of the Sodomites as having a sexual nature. It is certain he did not view their sin as inhospitality. Indeed, verse 8 speaks of the daily nature of their sinful acts. Are we to understand that daily the Sodomites showed inhospitality to strangers, or is it much more logical to realize that Lot was tormented by the constant homosexual lifestyle of the Sodomites, a lifestyle that brought God's eventual judgment?

Objection Stated

The story of Sodom and Gomorrah is irrelevant to homosexuality because it does not address loving, monogamous relationships. It is only decrying gang rape and violence, nothing else.

Biblical Response

Surely there is everything wrong with violence, whether sexual or not. And there is everything wrong with gang rape as well. But to note that these things are wrong does not explain many of the issues in the narrative of Genesis 19, as well as the rest of the Bible's references to Sodom and Gomorrah. There was no violence on the part of the crowd until Lot identified their desires as wicked. Was Lot wrong to identify homosexual desires for these men as wicked? And was Peter wrong to interpret the story from Genesis as involving daily ungodliness on the part of the Sodomites? Are we to assume the Sodomites engaged in daily gang rapes, or is it apparent that it was their lifestyle that tormented his soul?

The insertion of the concept of "monogamous, loving homosexual relationships" into the biblical discussion begs a number of issues. First, very few homosexual relationships are, in fact, monogamous. Second, to call a relationship "loving" in a biblical sense means it is in accordance with God's will and is fulfilling His purpose, resulting in His glory. And finally, it assumes that a homosexual relationship thusly described is part of the biblical concept to begin with, and such is an unfounded assertion refuted by the fair and careful examination of Scripture. Indeed, it is directly contrary to God's law, and to that truth we now turn.

Notes

1. The term is *sungenometha*, which is used in Genesis 39:10, and in the non-canonical book of Judith (12:16), in the same way.

2. Incredibly, many of the most popular works attempt to conflate these various arguments together, seemingly thinking that it is a matter of "the more, the merrier," not realizing that such a procedure results in hopeless confusion and contradiction.

3. Daniel Helminiak, *What the Bible Really Says About Homosexuality* (San Francisco: Alamo Square Press, 1995), 39–40.

4. Note as well that the same term, *abominations*, appears in verse 47, immediately before the point where Helminiak began his citation.

5. This is how it is used in such passages as Deuteronomy 29:23; 32:32; Isaiah 1:9–10; 3:9; 13:19; Jeremiah 49:18; 50:40; Lamentations 4:6; Amos 4:11; and Zephaniah 2:9.

CHAPTER THREE

Recycling the Older Testament: Introducing the Leviticus Passages

You shall not lie with a male as one lies with a female; it is an abomination. (Leviticus 18:22)

If there is a man who lies with a male as those who lie with a woman, both of them have committed a detestable act; they shall surely be put to death. Their bloodguiltiness is upon them. (Leviticus 20:13)

These verses are abundantly clear. Both passages unquestionably prohibit any type of same-sex intimacy and even prohibit the *interest* in same-sex intimacy. If God forbids certain deeds—declaring them sinful—we must necessarily conclude that the desire, the longing, or the interest in committing such deeds is sinful as well. One cannot say that although the deed of murder is sinful, the desire to murder is morally (and scripturally) acceptable;

therefore, from the outset, we can discard the attempted and unacceptable evasion that presents these passages as *only* dealing with homosexual acts and not with homosexual interest or desire.[1] The Bible, particularly these passages in Leviticus, prohibits homosexuality in both deed and desire.

Due to their clarity, these passages from Leviticus lie at the heart of the same-sex controversy that has come upon the church. The clarity of these verses is even recognized by those who advocate homosexuality as a biblically acceptable practice. Daniel A. Helminiak, in *What the Bible Really Says About Homosexuality*, after citing these Leviticus passages, admits, "This sounds pretty straightforward, and it sounds pretty bad."[2] Letha Scanzoni and Virginia Ramey Mollenkott, in *Is the Homosexual My Neighbor?* do not contest the clear import of these words: "Two Old Testament passages make explicit reference to homosexual acts."[3] John Boswell, in *Christianity, Social Tolerance, and Homosexuality*, also acknowledges the Leviticus passages as prohibitions against homosexual behavior.[4]

What do such revisionists do with these passages? How is it possible to avoid their clear teaching? For simplicity's sake, this chapter will summarize the multitude of revisions under two headings, and these will form the structure for the next two chapters. We will see that the Leviticus passages in question are either *rejected* for present-day applicability or are *revised* with regard to their historic context.

REJECTED:
THE LEVITICUS PASSAGES
DO NOT APPLY TO US

This approach recognizes the prohibitions against homosexuality that are found in the book of Leviticus and does not deny them, but these prohibitions, we are told, do not apply to the present day or current situation. Such claims are made because these prohibitions supposedly *only applied to the Jewish people of the Old Testament.* By restricting the Leviticus prohibitions in this way, this revision honestly admits the presence of the prohibition and so presents itself as "faithful" to the Bible. Those who take this approach admit that at some time, for some people, homosexuality was prohibited. Stated even more simply, homosexuality was forbidden *then and for them.*

This view speaks voluminously of matters that pertained to the external worship of the God of the Bible—the ceremonies of the Old Testament (sacrifices, the priesthood, the promised land, purity and cleanliness distinctions, dietary laws, etc.). These ceremonial aspects of the Old Testament Law will then be confused with regulations that are morally binding upon all people in all times. Such a conflation of the moral and ceremonial law[5] results in great misunderstanding. A lack of familiarity with the Old Testament can render one silent in the face of these assertions.

REVISED:
A RECYCLED PRESENTATION OF
"BIBLICAL BACKGROUNDS"

The second approach to reducing the Leviticus prohibitions to a non-applicable status is a bit more complex than the previous approach. Simply stated, Leviticus only prohibited a *particular type of homosexuality*: temple or cultic (religious) homosexuality, which was a form of homosexual prostitution. The adherents of this view arrive at their conclusions by (supposedly) allowing Scripture to interpret Scripture . . . all the while assuming that which they are trying to prove. They argue that the Leviticus prohibitions were *only* concerned with an idolatrous brand of homosexuality and not with the expression of same-sex intimacy that is "committed" and "loyal."

People who hold to the interpretive labyrinth of this view present it as a scholarly and complete understanding of the Bible, an approach that provides a handle on the historical situation and gives insights as to the cultural context.

IN SUMMARY

These revisions of the Leviticus passages are certainly creative but are woefully lacking in interpretive integrity. In the two chapters that follow, we will consider and respond to each of these evasions of the Leviticus prohibitions against homosexuality. The next chapter will be concerned with the attempt to reduce the prohibitions to something that is exclusively Jewish. The chapter following it will consider the strained approach that considers Leviticus to *only* prohibit religious homosexuality that is prostitution.

Once again, the controversy boils down to the authority of Scripture. As we look at these revisions of the clear teaching of God's Word in Leviticus, we will observe an approach to the interpretation of Scripture that is one of mere convenience. The interpretations offered are suited to the desires of those who are practicing, who long to practice, or those who are simply not opposed to the practice of same-sex intimacy. Clearly, the revisionists are concerned about the text of Leviticus. They are forced to be. To ignore these passages would allow the verses to accuse them and would thus reveal their dismissal of the clear teaching of the Bible.

Notes

1. Daniel Helminiak, in his book *What the Bible Really Says About Homosexuality*, observes the distinction between homosexual *acts* and homosexuality as an orientation. He coins a term that refers to homosexual acts; he calls this *homogenitality* (see pages 39–40). While a difference between deed and proclivity is obvious, recognizing a difference says nothing about the *morality* of a particular deed or desire.
2. *What the Bible Really Says About Homosexuality*, 51.
3. Letha Scanzoni and Virginia Ramey Mollenkott, *Is the Homosexual My Neighbor?* (San Francisco: HarperCollins, 1994), 60.
4. John Boswell, *Christianity, Social Tolerance, and Homosexuality* (Chicago: University of Chicago Press, 1980), 100–04.
5. In the next chapter we will consider this distinction between the moral and the ceremonial law.

CHAPTER FOUR

Recycling the Older Testament: The Leviticus Passages–Part One

You shall not lie with a male as one lies with a female; it is an abomination. (Leviticus 18:22)

If there is a man who lies with a male as those who lie with a woman, both of them have committed a detestable act; they shall surely be put to death. Their blood-guiltiness is upon them. (Leviticus 20:13)

These passages in the book of Leviticus are abundantly clear in their rejection of homosexuality as a practice or a proclivity. Homosexuality then and now is not compatible with biblical morality; it is not acceptable to God. Both sides of the same-sex controversy readily admit the clarity of these passages; therefore, those who advocate the acceptability of homosexuality in either deed or in desire must *do something* with these passages. They must answer the searing indictment from this portion of God's Word.

The first and most common approach to these passages by those who advocate the consistency of homosexuality with biblical morality is to present them as irrelevant to the discussion. This approach recognizes the prohibition against homosexuality in the book of Leviticus as real but argues that the prohibitions only applied *to the Jews of a previous era.* The argument claims that these proscriptions of Leviticus applied to the Jews of that day, not to us, and, therefore, ought not to be considered binding today. Usually someone utters the often used and misunderstood phrase, "After all, we are not under Law, but under grace." Let us consider the words of those who would dismiss the Leviticus passages in this way.

As we have seen, Daniel Helminiak, a Roman Catholic priest, has attempted, in part, to blunt the sharp edge of the Leviticus prohibitions by asserting the Jewish distinctiveness of these passages. According to Helminiak, the restrictions were something exclusively Jewish. He commented succinctly, "Not sex, but violation of Judaism is what was prohibited."[1] Previously he argued,

> The condemnation of homogenital acts occurs in a section of Leviticus called "The Holiness Code." This list of laws and punishments spells out requirements for Israel to remain "holy" in God's sight. . . . According to Jewish belief, Israel was God's "chosen people." Israel was bound to God by a covenant, a pact. That covenant required that the Israelites show themselves different from the other nations. They were God's People. They

were to maintain their own traditions. They were not to do things the way that other nations did. They needed to preserve their religious identity. . . . They now were to have nothing to do with the Gentiles. . . . So a main concern of The Holiness Code was to keep Israel different from the Gentiles. . . . *The point is that The Holiness Code of Leviticus prohibits male same-sex acts for religious reasons, not for sexual reasons. The concern is to keep Israel distinct from the Gentiles. Homogenital sex is forbidden because it is associated with Gentile identity. It departs from the Jewish understanding of how things should be.* (emphasis ours)[2]

Similarly, L. William Countryman, by relegating the prohibitions against homosexuality to (his understanding of) Israel's purity laws, conveniently concludes that they can only have reference to the Jews and Jewish culture of that time. Countryman said, "Every culture's purity law must be understood as expressing the culture's uniqueness as well as our common human interest in purity."[3] For Countryman, the Levitical opposition to homosexuality was a cultural matter. Rejecting the biblical standards of morality, he wrote,

For present purposes, it is enough to say that what marks particular sexual acts as violations of purity rather than of some other ethic is that the acts are deemed repellent in and of themselves, like snails or slugs on a dinner plate. One rejects them because they seem self-evidently unacceptable, not because of any identifiable concrete harm which they threaten to a society or to a person participating in them.[4]

The late John Boswell linked Leviticus's prohibitions of homosexuality to "those Jewish sins which involve ethnic contamination" and commented that the "manifest purpose" of Leviticus chapters 18 and 20 "is to elaborate a system of ritual 'cleanliness' whereby the Jew will be distinguished from neighboring peoples."[5]

And finally, Letha Scanzoni and Virginia Ramey Mollenkott argue that these prohibitions, while *previously* applicable to the Jews who received Leviticus, do not apply to us today since we do not follow other Levitical prescriptions and prohibitions. Their contention, at this point, is the classic "We are not under Law but under grace" argument. This argument is, by far, the most common employed by those who maintain that homosexuality is consistent with biblical morality. Typically, they make some reference to the Older Testament's dietary laws (Leviticus 11; Deuteronomy 14). For example, the Jews were not to eat pork or shellfish (Leviticus 11:7, 10–12). The argument is that since this legislation is not followed today, neither should we follow Leviticus when it comes to the prohibition of homosexuality. The case is supposedly closed. Scanzoni and Mollenkott present this type of argument as they comment on Leviticus 18:22 and 20:13:

> These verses are part of Israel's Holiness Code, which includes commandments not to eat meat with blood in it, not to wear garments made of two kinds of yarn, not to plant fields with two kinds of seed, and not to be tattooed, as well as specific instructions on sexual matters. Forbidden activities include bestiality (sexual

conduct with animals), incest (sexual conduct with relatives—children, parents, siblings, in-laws, and so on), male homosexual acts, adultery, and sexual intercourse with a woman during her menstrual period. The reasons given for these proscriptions involve several factors: (1) separation from other nations and their customs (Lev. 18:1–5), (2) avoidance of idolatry and any practices associated with it (Lev. 20:1–7), and (3) ceremonial uncleanness.[6]

Are the Leviticus prohibitions only commandments for the Jews of some previous day? Are we to see Leviticus 18:22 and 20:13 as mere cultural indicators that separated Israel from the surrounding nations? Is there a blatant inconsistency for Christians who believe that the Bible condemns homosexuality and then discuss such matters at dinner—over a rare steak while wearing a polyester blend garment? Are Christians in the contemporary church selective and hypocritical in their opposition to homosexuality since they do not offer animal sacrifices during the worship service and may happen to enjoy an occasional lobster dinner or eat ham during a holiday meal?

What response can be made to these arguments? The contention is that the prohibitions that are found in the book of Leviticus are arcane, obsolete, or inapplicable to the controversy before us. The truth of the matter is, however, that the condemnation of homosexuality as found in the book of Leviticus stands with present-day relevance— that homosexuality, then and now, was and is sinful and not approved by the Creator, the God of the Bible. The arguments offered to justify homosexuality as a biblically acceptable practice are scripturally indefensible.

ANSWERING THE EVASIONS AND REVISIONS

Even professing Christians encounter difficulties when they consider the book of Leviticus. Few people understand this third book of the Bible. Discussions become bogged down due to a lack of Bible reading and knowledge. Some people will make grandiose claims and bold assertions about the Law of God, about the book of Leviticus, and about "Holiness Codes" despite the fact that they are woefully misrepresenting the truth of God's Word (1 Timothy 1:7). A great deal of confusion could be avoided if those who bear the name of the Lord would spend more time reading the Bible. Often, this is enough to refute the revisionists' contentions.

Leviticus Only for the Jews?
A Case of Geographical Morality

Rabbi Jacob Milgrom has taught that the laws against homosexuality in the Old Testament were exclusively Jewish in scope and application. He has attempted to prove his point by going to the text of Leviticus and making reference to the land. He wrote,

The biblical prohibition is addressed only to Jews. Non-Jews are affected only if they reside in the Holy Land, but not elsewhere (see the closing exhortation in Leviticus 18, verses 24–30). Thus it is incorrect to apply this prohibition on a universal scale.[7]

The rabbi argues that making any universal application of these prohibitions is incorrect since they applied to the Jews and only to non-Jews if they resided in the Holy Land. This line of argumentation is an extreme case of "geographical morality." Essentially, Milgrom is arguing that homosexuality was wrong for an Egyptian if he resided in Judah, but it was not wrong if he lived in Egypt or Macedonia. Further questioning is required of this "geographical morality" position: Is it acceptable for a Jew to be a homosexual in New York, Denver, or Uganda, but not in Bethlehem? Although shocking with its situation ethic, this position is the argument of Rabbi Milgrom.

The misinformed rabbi cites Leviticus 18:24–30 and focuses on the defilement that will come upon the land due to the practice of homosexuality and from there draws his geographical conclusions. The passage in question reads as follows:

[24]Do not defile yourselves by any of these things; for by all these the nations which I am casting out before you have become defiled. [25]For the land has become defiled, therefore I have visited its punishment upon it, so the land has spewed out its inhabitants. [26]But as for you, you are to keep My statutes and My judgments, and

shall not do any of these abominations, neither the native, nor the alien who sojourns among you [27](for the men of the land who have been before you have done all these abominations, and the land has become defiled); [28]so that the land may not spew you out, should you defile it, as it has spewed out the nation which has been before you.

[29]For whoever does any of these abominations, those persons who do so shall be cut off from among their people. [30]Thus you are to keep My charge, that you do not practice any of the abominable customs which have been practiced before you, so as not to defile yourselves with them; I am the LORD your God.

The refutation of Milgrom's position is obvious upon reading the text of Leviticus. The very first thing that he misses is the fact that divine judgment had come upon the nations who previously dwelled in the land (see verses 25 and 27). Furthermore, these were nations that did not have the Law of God given to them on tablets of stone, yet God still held them responsible for their immoral behavior. Unquestionably, God's prohibition of homosexuality wasn't only a Jewish matter—it was something that transcended ethnic boundaries.[8]

Recognized as an authority on Leviticus, Milgrom reveals an odd selectivity with Leviticus and an apparent lack of thoroughness. Would he say that it would be acceptable (for anyone, Jew or Gentile) to sell one's daughter into harlotry while residing in Los Angeles? Or, would God's favor be upon the one who practiced incest while living in Argentina? We would hope that Milgrom would declare—in no uncertain terms—that such practices are immoral and reprehensible wherever they may occur, whatever the address or the locale. Furthermore, we would like to think that Milgrom's opposition to such practices stems from the fact that they are sinful—that God declares them so.

These are interesting questions, because the very same Law, the book of Leviticus, which Milgrom refers to, also teaches us that the selling of one's daughter into harlotry and the horrid practice of incest *also defiles the land* (Leviticus 19:29; 20:19–22). Will Rabbi Milgrom retain his geographical morality position? To teach that homosexuality is prohibited because it defiles the land, he must also conclude the same thing with regard to prostitution and incest. Will he strive to maintain some level of consistency? The clear reading of the Bible is refutation enough. The Leviticus prohibitions are not restricted to the Jews or to those who lived in the land.

Daniel Helminiak is wrong as well. Recall what he wrote concerning this passage in Leviticus 18: "The concern is to keep Israel distinct from the Gentiles. Homogenital sex is forbidden because it is associated with Gentile identity. It departs from the Jewish understanding of how things should be."[9] Rather, Helminiak departs from God's understanding of how things should be. Elsewhere he wrote,

> Evidently, the Jews of that pre-Christian era did not understand Leviticus to forbid male-male intercourse as

something wrong in itself. They understood Leviticus to forbid male-male intercourse as an offense against Jewish religion: it violated their understanding of the ideal order of creation, so it was Gentile-like, it was unjewish, it was dirty.[10]

On the contrary, the text of Leviticus 18:24–30 clearly reveals that God judged the *non-Jewish* nations who previously lived in the land because they violated His judgments and engaged in the type of sexual immorality that is listed in Leviticus 18:6–23.

After listing such practices as incest, intercourse during menstruation, adultery, offering one's children to Molech, homosexuality, and bestiality, Leviticus is abundantly clear: "Do not defile yourselves by *any of these things; for by all these the nations which I am casting out before you have become defiled.*" God, according to the clear teaching of the book of Leviticus, does not view "these things" (of which homosexuality is included) as something restricted to Jews so that they may demonstrate their Jewishness before other nations. Also, this passage states "for the men of the land who have been before you have done all these abominations." Clearly, these men "who have been before you" were not Jewish, and they had committed these deeds, these "abominations" (the very same word used to describe homosexuality in verse 22). The men who had lived in the land prior to the Hebrews had engaged in homosexual practices, and God judged them for it. God's disapprobation of homosexuality does not have ethical restrictions. As we have already seen, God judged the city of Sodom, in part, for their engagement in homosexuality, and the residents of Sodom were not Jewish. If God's prohibitions against homosexuality were restricted to the children of Israel, He would not have judged the surrounding nations for such sinfulness.

Leviticus and the Law—
Failing to Observe Biblical Distinctions

The most common attempt to reduce the Leviticus prohibitions of homosexuality to irrelevancy and view them as an exclusively Jewish matter is seen in the approach that conflates, confuses, and blurs various aspects of the Levitical law. Frequently, those who advocate the Bible's acceptance of homosexuality will argue their position by pointing out things that are contained in the book of Leviticus that are no longer practiced, or simply ignored, by those who profess to follow the God of the Bible. From this, it is often deduced that the book of Leviticus is no longer applicable to our contemporary situation. Those who advocate the compatibility of homosexuality and Christianity readily go to Leviticus and then challenge their challengers with a "What about this passage?" approach to obedience.

A few examples of this approach would be illustrative at this point. Scanzoni and Mollenkott have accused those who oppose their pro-homosexual position with scriptural inconsistency:

Consistency and fairness would seem to dictate that if the Holiness Code is to be invoked against twentieth-century homosexuals, it should likewise be invoked against such common practices as eating rare steak, wearing mixed fabrics, and having marital intercourse during the menstrual period.[11]

In a pamphlet titled "But Leviticus Says!" written by now retired homosexual pastor Fred L. Pattison, we find these words:

As we consider what is stated in Leviticus we need to observe that this Old Testament book has rules regarding what was to be eaten, type of clothing that was to be worn as well as a number of other areas of one's life including sexual restrictions. These were to be followed by the children of Israel. Nearly every area of Jewish life was spelled out in Leviticus. It should also be noted that Leviticus is a priestly book. It must be remembered that this book was addressed to the Jew living under the Old Covenant regulating their worship and living practices, both private and public. It must also be noted here that the regulations in eating, worship, wearing apparel, etc. are not literally binding upon we who live under Grace. We read in Romans 6:14 "For we are not under law but under grace." This does not mean that we are lawless. It simply means that the Law is complete and fulfilled in Christ (emphasis in the original).[12]

Later in this same pamphlet, Pattison continues his attempted "that was then and for them" evasion of the Leviticus passages:

Have you ever noticed how many people wear glasses? Some people wear contact lenses, nevertheless they still are wearing correctives for a needed correction in their eyesight. Ever noticed how many preachers wear glasses? Why don't we bar such people from attending our public gatherings? To do so would be scriptural. According to *Leviticus 21:16–23, "The* **LORD** *said to Moses, 'Say to Aaron: For the generations to come none of your descendants who has a defect may come near to offer the food of his God. No person who has ANY DEFECT may come near: no one who is BLIND OR LAME, DISFIGURED OR DEFORMED; NO ONE WITH A CRIPPLED FOOD [sic] OR HAND, OR WHO IS HUNCHBACKED OR DWARFED, OR WHO HAS ANY EYE DEFECT [glass wearers] or who has festering or running sores or damaged testicles"* (emphasis in the original).[13]

Contrary to his verse citation, Pattison did not quote through verse 23, but stopped after verse 20. It is interesting to see the conclusions he draws from such questions and Leviticus citations:

According to this passage there should be a screening out of who may and who may not come into the presence of the Lord in our public gatherings. This is scripture. *"But that's not for today?"*

Who says? If it is not to be applied to today's assembling why are the passages dealing with homosexuality said to apply? If the Levitical code is to be taken literally and applied today then the attendance at our public worship services would be cut drastically. Modern day churches do not carry out the prohibitions of Leviticus.

How is it possible for Christians to apply to small passages from Leviticus to homosexuals while at the same
time dismissing other portions of the book as not being
applicable for our day (emphasis in the original)?[14]

The argument essentially is, "If you do not obey *all* of
the book of Leviticus, then you cannot condemn me for
my disregard of 18:22 and 20:13." First of all, let it be
noted that a person's, or a nation's, obedience to God's
Word does not make a particular commandment valid or
binding. Those who are Christian strive to obey the Bible
where and when and how the Bible prescribes obedience,
regardless of popularity or opinion polls. Additionally,
ignorance of God's commands or redefinition of His commands does not give one a "not guilty" status before God.
Furthermore, those who argue from the book of Leviticus
as Pattison does reveal their ignorance of God's Word and
posture themselves as judges over God's own Word. In
their judgment over God's Word, they are adept at declaring when it is obligatory, when it is relevant, and when it
is applicable. Since they have confined the entire book of
Leviticus to an irrelevant, non-binding status, it can be disregarded in the present day.

To refer to the dietary laws of Leviticus 11, observing
that they are no longer practiced by Christians, does not
justify the disregard for God's Word concerning homosexuality in Leviticus. We must ask ourselves, "*Why* do we not
observe the dietary laws that God articulated in Leviticus?" The answer is simple. We do not observe the dietary

laws of Leviticus because God, in His own Word, has repealed them, and we know this from other passages in the Bible, not from our own preferences. The restrictions of eating shellfish, rock badger, or pork are no longer binding because Jesus removed them and declared all foods clean (Mark 7:19). The dietary laws were in place as a requirement upon the Jews as the covenant people of God. These *dietary* laws, not those concerning homosexuality, did serve, in part, to evidence the distinction between the Jews and other nations. In no place in the Bible do we read of God judging the surrounding nations for their failure to observe the dietary regulations—they were not required to do so. This function and these laws are no longer operable in the New Covenant era since such distinctions between Jew and Gentile are utterly abolished (see Acts 10; Ephesians 2:11–22; Galatians 3:28–29).

Where in the Bible has God abolished the prohibition against homosexuality? Nowhere! Though God has changed His Law with respect to the dietary regulations, and other matters that distinguished between the Jews and other nations (laws concerning the separation of fabrics and seed), He has not done so with homosexuality. We must not allow sexual preferences to interpret the Bible; the Bible is to interpret the Bible. Again, the pivotal concern is the authority of God's Word.

Pattison's quotation above, which selectively includes a portion of Leviticus 21 and refers to eyeglasses, physical handicaps, and deformities, does little to support his contention that the Bible and his homosexual lifestyle are compatible. The passage to which he refers is one that speaks *solely* of the Levitical high priest who must, by God's command, come from the lineage of Aaron (Leviticus 21:17, 21). The Levites who served in the sanctuary came from three families, all of the tribe of Levi: Kohath, Gershon, and Merari (Numbers 4; Exodus 6:16–19; 1 Chronicles 23:6). Aaron was a Kohathite, which provided some distinction between the role of high priest and the rest of the Levites (see Numbers 8, especially verse 19).

What is the significance of all of this? First, the passage clearly does nothing to support Pattison's strained points about Leviticus *as a whole* no longer being applicable. Once we allow the Bible to interpret the Bible, we see that the high priesthood is no longer operative because Jesus is our final and perfect High Priest (Hebrews 2:17; 3:1; 4:14–16; 5:5; 6:20; 7:1–8:4; 9:24–28; 10:11–14). The Aaronic and Levitical priesthood is no longer. The high priests of the Older Testament were temporary, pointing forward to the one final and perfect High Priest, Jesus Christ (Hebrews 7:14–28). The High Priesthood of Jesus has done away with the previous priesthood, and the book of Hebrews unquestioningly demonstrates this point.

Even more, this fact reveals the rationale behind the requirement that the Aaronic high priest be without defect (not sinless), since he was prefiguring the perfect High Priest who was to come. Simply stated, the restrictions that pertain to physical deformities and handicaps had nothing to do with moral or immoral behavior. Persons with such conditions were still allowed to worship;

they simply could not function as the high priest. Such restrictions did not apply to every person; they applied only to the high priest who had to be a descendent of Aaron and whose office pointed forward to the coming Redeemer.

So, a *certain portion* of the book of Leviticus (legislation regarding the high priest) is no longer binding, because God, in His Word and according to His purpose, has rendered the Levitical high priesthood inoperative. This realization, however, is quite a different matter than determining, on the basis of one's own presumed authority, that the *entirety* of the book of Leviticus is irrelevant today. Many portions of the book of Leviticus are perpetually obligatory. Leviticus 18:20 forbids adultery and 19:4 prohibits idolatry. We are still required to love one another (Leviticus 19:9–18), and Jesus himself quoted Leviticus 19:18 in Matthew 19:19 and 22:39. Today it is commonly asked, "What would Jesus do?" Clearly, one of the things that Jesus would do is quote Leviticus.

Again the question looms before us, "Where or when has God changed in His moral disapprobation of homosexuality?" Are there portions of the book of Leviticus that no longer apply to us today? Yes. But these are to be determined by God's Word, not lustful passions or sexual experimentation. God's Word is binding—all of it. It is obligatory at every point in which it declares itself to be. Since God is the One who gave His Word (in this case, the Law), He is the only One who has the right to annul or repeal it.

Returning the Challenge—
Leviticus, Bestiality, and Pedophilia

Those who propose that we no longer consider the Leviticus prohibitions of homosexuality as binding must tell us what is to be done with the rest of the book. They are left in the inconsistent position of either rejecting it all (which Jesus did not do, as seen in Matthew 22:39—Jesus citing Leviticus 19:18) or revealing their true colors and showing their own subjectively selective approach to biblical interpretation.

We *can* discern what is permanent and what is temporary in God's Word. If God has not repealed His Law at any given point, His Law stands, which poses a problem for those advocating the acceptability of homosexuality with the Bible, for they must answer why bestiality and pedophilia are moral evils. Such practices are sinful because God declares them so. Specifically, bestiality is condemned in Leviticus 18:23, just one verse after the first Leviticus prohibition of homosexuality, and yet *nowhere else outside of the Law of Moses* is bestiality mentioned (Exodus 22:19; Leviticus 20:15; Deuteronomy 27:21). Recognizing that the Pentateuch was originally delivered to Israel, is the prohibition against intimacy with a beast applicable today to persons outside of Israel? Why is bestiality wrong today?

L. William Countryman has attempted an answer to this question. As is typical with like interpreters, a complex flurry of suggestions are offered, perhaps aimed at giving the impression that a number of possible answers exist.

Countryman, after noting the close proximity of the prohibitions against homosexuality in 18:22 and bestiality in
18:23, suggests these "may have been connected only as
examples of 'confusion' or as relatively rare or unusual
violations of purity in contrast to the more everyday problems occasioned by marriage and family life."[15] Confusion, indeed. As noted earlier, Countryman has taught
that purity concerns in the book of Leviticus are simply a
matter of cultural taste and toleration, "like snails or slugs
on a dinner plate." It is interesting, also, that Countryman
nowhere denounces the practice of bestiality; it is just
assumed to be immoral.

More than mere cultural notions of impurity are connected with bestiality, so Countryman offers another possible explanation. Again, due to the close proximity of homosexuality and bestiality in the text of the Bible, he writes,
"They may have shared another feature, an association with
idolatry."[16] He notes how bestiality also is condemned in
the book of Exodus and that this prohibition is connected
with sorcery and idolatry (Exodus 22:18–22).

Countryman takes these three practices—homosexuality, bestiality, and sorcery—and concludes that they may
be wrong because of their connection with idolatry: "The
theme that links the three elements is their association
with non-Israelite cultus (i.e., religious practice). . . . The
author may well have regarded both homosexual acts and
bestiality as tainted with idolatry."[17]

Although we will be dealing with this particular evasion
of the Leviticus prohibitions of homosexuality in more

detail in the next chapter, the refutation of it is actually quite simple. Simply remove the idolatry and religious ("cultus") aspects from the practice, and then ask if the behavior is acceptable. Remove the idolatry from the sorcery: does it become moral? Remove the idolatry from bestiality; consider it to be practiced in a "non-religious" way. Does that make it acceptable before God? We can take the same approach to adultery or prostitution. Do these practices become acceptable when they are practiced non-religiously, away from the temple? The answers are obvious: God condemns them in the temple and in the town, in the church and in society. Whatever God condemns, whatever He prohibits, is prohibited because it is contrary to His perfect holiness. To practice sins in a religious context—to add idolatry to certain sins—only compounds the sin.

Another disturbing topic to consider in this regard is pedophilia. The authors have no desire to engage in a discussion of graphic sins simply for shock value. We present this topic because of the similarity of argumentation that can be used to justify sexual relations with a child as with those that are being offered to justify homosexuality. Let us be perfectly clear, we are not accusing homosexuals of being child molesters. On the contrary, we wish to highlight the inconsistency of a homosexual's adherence to a line of argumentation that many of them would find repugnant when used by those who wish to support pedophilia.

Though we strenuously disagree, many homosexuals will argue that the Bible *nowhere* condemns homosexuality and that, therefore, homosexuality must be a biblically acceptable lifestyle today. How does this line of reasoning stand up when it comes to pedophilia? Where is the verse that condemns it? The Bible unquestioningly condemns incest (Leviticus 18), and that would include the child members of one's own family. So, as far as the biblical prohibition of incest is concerned, pedophilia is prohibited in one's own family. But what about the practice of pedophilia with someone who does not belong to your family? Would this form of pedophilia be acceptable?

Most people (we hope) would say that this practice is not acceptable; however, we must ask, where is the Bible verse that prohibits this practice of child intimacy? If it doesn't exist, then what is to prevent this horrid practice? This uncomfortable reasoning is precisely the problem for those claiming that the Bible does not condemn or prohibit homosexuality. They claim that the Bible does not provide a single verse that prohibits the practice, so it must be acceptable.[18] This type of faulty reasoning is a slippery slope into hell. Such is the outcome of the attempt to render Leviticus obsolete.

The Moral and Ceremonial Laws Distinguished

The chief failure of those who reduce the book of Leviticus to a non-applicable status is in not recognizing the proper biblical distinctions between that which God intended to be temporary and that which is permanent and applicable to all persons. The Bible does make distinctions between what was temporary, solely intended for the children of Israel, and that which is universal, unchanging, and obligatory upon all peoples in all places.

We have not denied that parts of the book of Leviticus offer temporary instruction. Some regulations are no longer observed due to divine amendment. We have already seen this to be the case with regard to the dietary laws and the ordinances that pertained to the priesthood. Bible scholars and theologians have recognized these distinctions and categorized them as the *ceremonial* and *moral* law.[19] God's moral law refers to those precepts that are perpetually binding upon all peoples in all time (murder, adultery, the sole worship of the One true God). God's ceremonial law refers to those precepts (ordinances, regulations) that were temporarily in effect and were specifically designed for the worship of God by His covenant people. These temporary statutes, in part, pointed forward to (prefigured) the person and work of the Messiah, Jesus Christ (the priesthood, the tabernacle, temple, sacrifices, Passover, and the feasts) as well as referred to those aspects of divine requirement that pertained only to those persons who were "in covenant" with the Lord. These ceremonial laws *were* temporary in practice and in design.[20]

The ceremonial laws also pertained to practices that were intended to *distinguish* the people of Israel from other nations. The ceremonial law included such matters as the sacrifices, the priesthood, the tabernacle, and (later) the temple, the offerings, and the festival calendar, which included Passover and the Day of Atonement. These practices, distinctive to Israel, would also include the regulations regarding the blending of fabrics, seed, and cattle as well as those that pertained to trimming of the hair and beards— Israel was a distinct nation (Exodus 19:5; Leviticus 11:44–47; Deuteronomy 4:5–8; 7:6–11). To illustrate the difference between the ceremonial law and the moral law, note that no Egyptian, Assyrian, Moabite, or Edomite was ever condemned for missing Passover or for not following the dietary laws or ignoring beard-trimming regulations. Furthermore, Passover was *only* for those who were already marked by the covenant sign of circumcision (Exodus 12:43–51). Passover was not required of those who were not followers of the Lord. The same could be said of the sacrifices, the priesthood, the festival calendar—none of these things were required of those outside of Israel.

The ceremonial law, since it was concerned with the Old Covenant worship of God and the duties of those involved in worship, prefigured the person and work of Christ, and is sometimes called the "restorative" or "redemptive" law. It is called this not because it provided redemption but because it *explained* or *illustrated* the way of redemption. The Law was never intended to provide salvation (Galatians 2:21; 3:21). Salvation has always been by grace and through faith and based upon the perfect work of Jesus Christ.

Excursus

The Distinction Between the Ceremonial and Moral Law As Necessary for Biblical Interpretation

Recognizing this distinction between the ceremonial and moral law is vitally important in properly understanding such passages as 1 Samuel 15:22: "Has the LORD as much delight in burnt offerings and sacrifices as in obeying the voice of the LORD? Behold, to obey is better than sacrifice, and to heed than the fat of rams." The Lord has commanded of His covenant people adherence to both His moral and His ceremonial law; however, in this passage, obedience "is *better* than sacrifice." How can this be since God has commanded both? The answer is that, even for the children of Israel who were commanded to offer sacrifices in accordance with the ceremonial law that regulated their lives and worship, loyalty to the Lord by obeying His moral law came first. Persons who disregarded the commandments of God's moral law were not welcome to present their offerings. This fact is clearly seen in Psalm 40:

> Sacrifice and meal offering Thou has not desired; my ears Thou hast opened; burnt offering and sin offering Thou hast not required. Then I said, "Behold, I come; in the scroll of the book it is written of me; I delight to do Thy will, O my God; Thy law is within my heart" (vv. 6–8).

The psalmist declares that God "does not desire" sacrifice and meal offering, burnt offering, and sin offering. How can this be when God has commanded such offerings to be brought to Him? The worshiper is not allowed, in either the Old or New Testament, to come before the Lord in some stale, perfunctory manner without regard for obedience: "I delight to do Thy will, O my God." This is seen in Psalm 51 as well:

> For Thou dost not delight in sacrifice, otherwise I would give it; Thou are not pleased with burnt offering. The sacrifices of God are a broken spirit; a broken and contrite heart, O God, Thou wilt not despise. By Thy favor do good to Zion; build the walls of Jerusalem. Then Thou will delight in righteous sacrifices, in burnt offering and whole burnt offering; then young bulls will be offered on Thine altar. (vv. 16–19)

The Lord desires "righteous sacrifices" offered by one whose heart is broken and contrite—by one who is striving after righteousness. God desires adherence to His moral law before ceremonial offerings are made. Those who reject or disregard God's moral requirements are unwelcome in worship. For this reason, Proverbs 15:8 and 21:27 teach: "The sacrifice of the wicked is an abomination to the LORD." Later, in Proverbs 28:9, we read, "He who turns away his ear from listening to the law, even his prayer is an abomination." The Lord, through the prophet Amos, who primarily rebuked the northern kingdom of Israel, also rejected the religious offerings of His people because of their disobedience.

> I hate, I reject your festivals, nor do I delight in your solemn assemblies. Even though you offer up to Me burnt offerings and your grain offerings, I will not accept them. And I will not even look at the peace offerings of your fatlings. Take away from Me the noise

of your songs; I will not even listen to the sound of your harps. But let justice roll down like waters and righteousness like an ever-flowing stream. (Amos 5:21–24)

The distinction between the ceremonial and moral law is one that is made in the Bible; it is not something that has been foisted upon the text of Scripture. Recognizing such a distinction allows us to properly interpret the Bible. In conclusion, one author stated the matter this way:

> The defender of homosexuality must produce a viable criterion for distinguishing between the moral and ceremonial laws, or else consistently reject them all (contrary to the emphatic word of Christ). We have New Testament warrant for discontinuing the sacrificial system (Hebrews 10:1–18), and the failure to observe the symbols of separation from the Gentile no longer displeases God (Acts 10:9–20). However, the Scriptures never alter God's revealed law regarding homosexuality, but leave us under its full requirement (Deuteronomy 8:3; 12:32; Matthew 4:4). Indeed, the Bible repeatedly condemns homosexuality, the New Testament itself stressing that it is contrary to God's law (1 Timothy 1:9–10), bringing God's judgment and exclusion from the kingdom (Romans 1:24 ff; 1 Corinthians 6:9–10). Therefore, the prohibition against homosexuality cannot be viewed as part of the ceremonial system prefiguring Christ or as temporary in its obligation.[21]

The moral law, on the other hand, referred to those aspects of divine requirement that were binding upon all peoples, in all places, and in all times. Murder looked like murder before and after the Law was given. Idolatry, murder, adultery, homosexuality, covetousness, and theft all look pretty much the same from Creation to today. As a matter of biblical record, Peter refers to the sins of Sodom and Gomorrah as *"lawless* deeds" (2 Peter 2:8). Their deeds, committed before the Law was given on Sinai and before Abraham was made into a great nation, are described as *lawless,* illustrating the operative presence of God's Law in the world long before Moses. For this reason, some people refer to the moral law as "Creation law."[22] In contrast to the ceremonial law, which was *not* required of the nations that surrounded Israel,[23] the moral law *is* required of both Israel *and* the nations that surrounded it. The Bible is unambiguous on this point. As far as this discussion is concerned, one of the ways that we are able to biblically distinguish between the ceremonial and moral precepts of God's Law is to recognize that the moral law was required of persons outside of Israel.

To whom did the prophet Obadiah address his prophecy of imminent judgment? To Edom. To whom did the prophet Jonah eventually warn of God's judgment? Ninevah. The prophet Nahum also addressed Ninevah. The prophets Isaiah, Jeremiah, and Ezekiel addressed several of the nations that surrounded Israel (Isaiah 13–23; Jeremiah 46–51; Ezekiel 25–32). One will search in vain for a word of God's judgment upon these nations for failing to make it to Jerusalem in order to offer their sacrifices. God's judgment upon them is in accordance with His moral, Creation law, not His ceremonial law.

We also learn to recognize the distinction between the

ceremonial and moral aspects of God's Law by their permanence. Was the legislation temporary, or was it permanent? To answer the question, determine whether the legislation in any way pointed forward to, or prefigured, the person and work of the Messiah who was to come. Those requirements that pointed forward to the person and work of the coming Messiah had to be, by definition, temporary. So what practices were temporary and prefiguring? The sacrificial system, for example, qualifies (Hebrews 10), the tabernacle and the temple clearly qualify (Hebrews 3:6; 1 Peter 2:5; John 1:14), and, finally, as we have already noted, the priesthood most certainly qualifies (one of the main arguments of the book of Hebrews). In what way did God's legislation regarding homosexuality point forward to, or prefigure, the Messiah who was to come? It did not in any way. This deduction is one way that enables us to recognize God's prohibition of homosexuality as a moral law and not a temporary, ceremonial one. In addition, one more very significant matter in Scripture firms up the category into which laws against homosexuality must fall: the death penalty.

THE DEATH PENALTY AND THE LAW— MORAL OR CEREMONIAL?

Homosexuality, in some cases in Scripture, called for the death penalty. Despite the fact that such a definitive judgment would stand against those who are in violation of this portion of the Bible's standards of morality, those who claim that the Bible and homosexuality are compatible often introduce the death penalty into the discussion.

The death penalty for homosexuality is found in Leviticus 20:13: "If there is a man who lies with a male as those who lie with a woman, both of them have committed a detestable act; they shall surely be put to death. Their bloodguiltiness is upon them." From verses such as this one, it is not difficult to see why Leviticus must be, for some, removed from the discussion. For other homosexual advocates within the church, however, the death penalty is actually brought up as an attempt to win the argument. After all, who would advocate the death penalty against practicing homosexuals today? It is not uncommon for anyone who dares to affirm such a passage from the Bible to be accused of being antiquated, from the backwater, or filled with hate.

The first point to keep in mind is that those who argue in this way are actually contending against the God of the Bible. It is God who has determined that some offenses of homosexuality deserve the death penalty, not the person who is the messenger of God's truth. This divinely appointed penalty is applicable in both the Old and New Testaments. The apostle Paul taught that homosexuality deserved the death penalty as well (Romans 1:24–32).

The next point that we need to remember is that the Bible did not require the execution of *every known homosexual*. The rhetoric often flashes about in this way: "Oh, so you want to kill all the gays." No. That would be unbiblical too. During the reign of Asa, King of Judah, he is described as one who "did what was right in the sight of the LORD. . . . He also put away the male cult prostitutes from the land, and removed all the idols which his fathers had made" (1 Kings 15:11–12). Asa received divine approbation because he removed the homosexual cult prostitutes. Notice that these homosexuals were not executed; as a matter of fact, they were not completely eradicated from the land.

During the reign of Jehoshaphat, Asa's son, we find him picking up where his father left off: "And the remnant of the sodomites who remained in the days of his father Asa, he expelled from the land" (1 Kings 22:46). Again, we see that they were not summarily executed, but over an extended period of time—through the reigns of his father and into his own reign—they worked on ridding the land of this sinful practice. Those who wanted to remain among the covenant people of the Lord were required to repent.

Two hundred years later, we find Josiah, in the midst of a reform, doing the exact same thing: "He also broke down the houses of the male cult prostitutes which were in the house of the LORD" (2 Kings 23:7).

Despite these exceptions, the Bible does allow for the execution of homosexuals. This sanction is taught in the book of Leviticus and is implemented by God upon the residents of Sodom (Genesis 19). We may safely conclude that in both precept and in practice God allows for the maximum penalty to be applied to unrepentant homosexuals. What's the point? *Not a single application of the death penalty to the general citizenry of Israel existed for violation of a*

ceremonial law.[24] This fact unquestionably places God's prohibition of homosexuality in the category of moral law,
obligatory upon all peoples in all places. God nowhere
prescribed death as a possible penalty for those who
refused to circumcise their sons,[25] mixed their fabrics,
missed a Passover meal, or failed to make it to Jerusalem
for one of the three required annual feasts. These persons
were excommunicated; they were to be "cut off" from
among the people, but they were not put to death. Present-day homosexuals disagree with the biblical provision
of the death penalty being enacted upon them for their
practices, but, in fact, few of them would consent to being
excommunicated from the church either.

Also important to note is that the Bible allows for the
execution of homosexuals by a godly and just civil government, *not* the church. The Bible does not sanction
ungodly means, such as entrapment or stalking, to accomplish this end. The subject of homosexuality is an emotional issue in our day. It probably was during the time of
the Old Testament as well. While it is likely that the emo-
tions have remained the same, our standards for morality,
sadly, have not; therefore, not only has confusion over the
acceptance of homosexuality proliferated but so also has
confusion over how to react to homosexuals.[26]

In summary

Clearly, we cannot simply scrap the book of Leviticus. We
need to learn to make distinctions where the Bible makes

distinctions. The entirety of Leviticus is not applicable today, neither is all of it inapplicable. We must allow the Bible to interpret itself. We have seen that the attempts offered to reduce the prohibitions against homosexuality in the book of Leviticus to something that is exclusively Jewish are without warrant and will not stand up to biblical scrutiny. It is far too simplistic to assert that we "are not under law, but under grace" (Romans 6:14) as if the law had no relevance for the Christian today. Paul, who frequently cites the law as he is teaching the church (even the Gentile churches), quotes from Leviticus and many other portions of the Law of Moses. Paul must have meant something other than "the law is irrelevant" when he wrote those oft-misunderstood words in Romans 6:14 (see appendix A, where we consider the relationship between law and grace).

At least one more serious attempt to reduce the book of Leviticus to non-applicable status in the present controversy over homosexuality remains. This one, too, will fail to provide what its proponents claim. We will look at this in the next chapter.

Notes

1. *What the Bible Really Says About Homosexuality*, 55.
2. Ibid., 53–54.
3. L. William Countryman, *Dirt, Greed, and Sex: Sexual Ethics in the New Testament and Their Implications for Today* (Minneapolis: Augsburg Fortress, 1988), 13. Countryman's first two chapters are concerned to develop the notion (*his* notion) of the purity laws of Israel. It is absolutely essential, for his argument in favor of homosexual practice and interest to be maintained, that he set the terms of purity to be something exclusively Jewish without *any* application to the nations or people surrounding Israel. This way, he can present the Leviticus prohibitions as irrelevant to the contemporary discussion and, therefore, he concludes, must be brushed aside.
4. Ibid., 18.
5. *Christianity, Social Tolerance, and Homosexuality*, 100.
6. *Is the Homosexual My Neighbor*, 60.
7. "Does the Bible Prohibit Homosexuality?" *Bible Review*, December 1993. This argument is also espoused by Dr. Joseph A. Pearson in his pro-homosexual video series, *Christianity and Homosexuality (Reconciled)*. L. William Countryman teaches something very similar in his book *Dirt, Greed, and Sex*, 40.
8. Later in this chapter, we will consider the biblical teaching that God's moral law has been obligatory upon all peoples in all times.
9. *What the Bible Really Says About Homosexuality*, 54–55.
10. Ibid., 65.
11. *Is the Homosexual My Neighbor*, 60–61.

12. Fred L. Pattison, "But Leviticus Says!" (Phoenix: Cristo Press, 1993), 8–9.

13. Ibid., 15.

14. Ibid., 15–16.

15. *Dirt, Greed, and Sex*, 33.

16. Ibid., 33. A couple of other "associations" that these three sins have in common and are conveniently overlooked by Countryman are that they are violations of God's Law and they (all three) called for the death penalty.

17. Ibid.

18. The biblical case against pedophilia is not dependent upon a specific commandment that uses *exact* words such as "Thou shalt not" followed by some reference to intimacy with children. The Bible, in teaching about God's institution of marriage, has set the boundaries of sexual intimacy as something that is to occur between a man and his wife. Marriage, by God's design, precludes pedophilia. Sexual intimacy outside of God's prescription is considered fornication or adultery.

19. See Walter C. Kaiser, *Toward an Old Testament Theology* (Grand Rapids: Zondervan, 1978), 114–19, and John Colquhoun, *A Treatise on the Law and the Gospel*, First American Edition, 1835, reprinted by Soli Deo Gloria, 1999. Also see William Einwechter, *Ethics and God's Law: An Introduction to Theonomy* (Mill Hall, Penn.: Preston/Speed, 1995).

20. The *London Baptist Confession* of 1689 explained the distinction in this way: "Besides the moral law God also gave to the people of Israel ceremonial laws which served as types of things to come. They fell into two main groups. In one group were rites, partly relating to worship, which pre-figured Christ, His graces, actions, sufferings, and the blessing He procured for us. The other group contained a variety of instructions about moral duties. By divine appointment all

these ceremonial laws were to be observed, but only until they were abrogated in New Testament days by Jesus Christ, the true Messiah and only law-giver, who was empowered by the Father to terminate them" (chapter 19). Prior to the London Baptist Confession, this same understanding of the distinction between the moral and ceremonial law is found in chapter 19 of the *Westminster Confession of Faith* (1647/48).

In a section of the *Westminster Confession of Faith*, we find this helpful explanation of the distinction between the Old and New Testament administrations: "This covenant was differently administered in the time of the law, and in the time of the gospel: under the law it was administered by promises, prophecies, sacrifices, circumcision, the paschal lamb, and other types and ordinances delivered to the people of the Jews, all foresignifying Christ to come: which were, for that time, sufficient and efficacious, through the operation of the Spirit, to instruct and build up the elect in faith in the promised Messiah, by whom they had full remission of sins, and eternal salvation; and is called the Old Testament" (chapter 7, paragraph 5).

"Under the gospel, when Christ, the substance, was exhibited, the ordinance in which this covenant is dispensed are the preaching of the Word, and the administrations of the sacraments of Baptism and the Lord's Supper: which, though fewer in number, and administered with more simplicity, and less outward glory; yet, in them, it is held forth in more fullness, evidence, and spiritual efficacy, to all nations, both Jews and Gentiles; and is called the New Testament. There are not therefore two covenants of grace, differing in substance, but one and the same, under various dispensations" (chapter 7, paragraph 6).

21. Greg L. Bahnsen, *Homosexuality: A Biblical View* (Grand Rapids: Baker Book House 1991), 40–41.

22. Douglas Wilson, sermon series on the Ten Commandments.

23. In Deuteronomy 14:21 we read of God's prohibition for the children of Israel; they are not to eat "anything which dies of itself," something in which the cause of death is not direct, such as slaying for the purpose of eating. The Israelites, however, are allowed to give such an animal to a non-Israelite. The same regulation is found in Leviticus 7:24. This clearly shows an example of a ceremonial law, one that is *solely* for Israel (a dietary law, in this case).

24. Some may want to argue at this point that violation of the Sabbath of the Fourth Commandment would be an instance of the death penalty being applied in the case of violating a *ceremonial* law, but this is a misunderstanding of the Sabbath commandment. The Fourth Commandment, being part of the Ten Words, the Decalogue, is not primarily a ceremonial law; it is chiefly a moral law. The Sabbath was obligatory *prior* to the law of ceremonies being given on Sinai (see Genesis 2:2–3; Exodus 16:29; 20:11), and Jesus taught us that the Sabbath was made for man (kind), not just for Jews (Mark 2:27). We do not deny that there were ceremonial elements associated with Sabbath observance from Sinai on—sacrifices, etc. (see Numbers 28)— but this does not render the Sabbath of the Fourth Commandment *entirely* ceremonial. There were ceremonial aspects associated with other commandments as well—this does not make them entirely ceremonial (see the Fifth Commandment with the ongoing requirement to honor father and mother—Ephesians 6:1–3—without reference to the ceremonial aspect of land; Exodus 20:12 and Deuteronomy 5:16). Moral commandments sometimes have ceremonial elements attached to them.

25. Some may want to argue that the Lord's desire to kill Moses for

his failure to circumcise his son (Exodus 4:24) is an instance of the death penalty for a transgression of a ceremonial law. Such is not the case. To reason in this way, first of all, reveals a failure to distinguish between that which Israel was to do among the people (punishments enacted judicially, man to man) and that which God himself (directly) may do. The prescribed penalty for failing (refusal) to circumcise one's sons was excommunication, not death (Genesis 17:14). Futhermore, this reveals a failure to recognize the distinction between *leaders* among the congregation of Israel and the *general citizenry* of Israel. To be sure, there were requirements upon the leaders that were not upon the people as a whole. The failure of a leader to follow some of these requirements could result in death (Nadab and Abihu, Leviticus 10). Moses was distinctive as a leader among the people (Numbers 12) and, as such, much was required of him.

26. The consideration of capital crimes according to the Bible—not merely by a government, but by a godly and just civil government—is complex and not capable of easy answers. This topic must be pursued according to biblical standards of morality. God requires all persons to perform their duties in accordance with His moral standards, including judges and magistrates. This requires that we be people who search the Word of God for wisdom in the application of God's moral precepts. Suspicion is not enough. Personal preferences are not enough. All people must be granted fairness, and fairness must be defined by the Word of God (due process, multiple and credible witnesses, for the protection of society, etc.). Government officials have been appointed by God to impose sanctions on those who do evil (Romans 13:1–5). This is a moral duty that requires that God's standards be known and followed. It is required of civil officials that they search the Scriptures, do careful exegesis, pursue thorough discussion, and even debate the matter before applying God's standards of justice to society.

CHAPTER FIVE

Recycling the Older Testament: The Leviticus Passages–Part Two

You shall not lie with a male as one lies with a female; it is an abomination. (Leviticus 18:22)

If there is a man who lies with a male as those who lie with a woman, both of them have committed a detestable act; they shall surely be put to death. Their bloodguiltiness is upon them. (Leviticus 20:13)

Another approach that strives to evade the clear teaching of the Leviticus passages that prohibit homosexuality focuses on the historical context and the biblical background, asserting that once these are properly understood, people will see that the Leviticus passages do not condemn homosexuality as we know it today. These passages do, according to these revisionists, condemn homosexuality *of a particular kind.* They claim that once we allow

Scripture to interpret Scripture, the Bible simply *does not condemn every form or expression* of homosexuality. This claim holds that the homosexuality that is prohibited in the Leviticus context was an expression of homosexuality that was somehow linked to religious practices. The Bible does reference and thoroughly condemn those who practice homosexuality in a religious or idolatrous manner, usually in a context of religious or temple prostitution. The difficulty is that these revisionists are claiming that this type of homosexuality is the only type being prohibited by Leviticus.

Their argument typically contends that the Bible allows for heterosexual expressions of love and homosexual expression of love (which is their assumption). Just as it is defiling to practice heterosexual love in an idolatrous manner as part of one's religious devotion or with a temple prostitute, they say, so too it is wrong to practice homosexual love in such a context. Their reasoning continues in this manner: "It is just as wrong for a heterosexual male to visit a female cult (religious) prostitute as it is for a homosexual male to visit a male cult prostitute."

Letting the Revisionists Speak for Themselves

L. William Countryman speaks of this religious expression of homosexuality as he refers to the writer of the book of

Leviticus: "The author may well have regarded . . . homosexual acts . . . as tainted with idolatry."[1]

Scanzoni and Mollenkott argue similarly in their book
Is the Homosexual My Neighbor? They write,

> Most scholars agree that in the fertility religions of
> Israel's neighbors, male cult prostitutes were employed
> for homosexual acts. The people who loved and served
> the God of Israel were strictly forbidden to have any-
> thing to do with such idolatry, and Jewish men were
> commanded never to serve as temple prostitutes (Deut.
> 23:17–19; 1 Kings 14:24; 2 Kings 23:7).[2]

Charles Coppinger, a former chaplain of the Arizona
State Legislature, ousted when he revealed that he was
homosexual, has commented, "The verses most people
cite regarding homosexuality actually speak of sexual
immorality, idolatry, inhospitality, and promiscuity. They
are silent regarding monogamous, loving, committed,
same-sex relationships."[3]

Dr. Joseph A. Pearson, in his video series *Christianity
and Homosexuality (Reconciled),* points out this same connection between homosexuality and idolatry in Leviticus and
1 Kings. This connection is, according to these revisionists,
solely a connection between idolatry and homosexuality.
Pearson recognizes that Leviticus 18:22 and 20:13 refer to
homosexuality, and he also admits that God drove out the
nations who were in the land before Israel, in part for
their homosexual practices. Driven out for what kind of
homosexual practice? Was it just any and every expression

of homosexuality? Not according to the revisionists.

Pearson refers to 1 Kings 14 and points out that the "sodomites" (KJV), or "male cult prostitutes" (NASB), were then in the land during Rehoboam's reign. He then cites verse 24: "They [the sodomites] did according to all the abominations of the nations which the LORD dispossessed before the sons of Israel." The abominations included temple cult prostitution, homosexuality of an idolatrous nature. Pearson, with a peek into biblical backgrounds, has shown us that 1 Kings 14:24 is pointing back to that which is referenced by the book of Leviticus. The homosexual temple prostitutes were plying their trade "according to all the abominations of the nations, which the LORD had dispossessed before the sons of Israel." Pearson explains,

> Had homosexuality been the reason that the Lord had cast out the nation before the children of Israel, he would not have referred specifically to male temple cult prostitution in 1 Kings 14:24. Thus, we are provided, in 1 Kings 14:24, with an important—a very important—interpretive link to Leviticus 18:22: that God is referring to male-male sex in the context of temple cult prostitution. Further, in Leviticus 18:21–24, all four verses must be taken together: "For by these things."[4]

If the biblical background can be colored in accordance with the revisionists' desires, then the prohibitions against homosexuality will look sensible in their time and context but appear ridiculous in ours. The revisionists

happily declare their consonance with the biblical prohibitions, stating that they, too, are opposed to this type of
homosexual expression. This approach, however, is an
attempt at evading the Leviticus prohibitions. It gives the
impression of being scholarly and of allowing the Bible to
interpret the Bible. It claims to recognize and honor the
Levitical prohibitions while supposedly digging just a bit
deeper than others. It attempts to show that the prohibitions against homosexuality in the Bible are prohibitions
that *only* concern the practice of same-sex intimacy as cultic, religious prostitution, which is idolatrous.

ANSWERING THIS EVASION

The first point to note in response to this attempted evasion of God's clear Word is that the revisionists are assuming that which they are trying to prove. Throughout their
argumentation they assume the moral acceptability of
some type of homosexuality. They assume that God
approves of *some expression* of homosexuality as a legitimate
sexual preference, just so long as it is not tainted by idolatry. This stance is question-begging in the extreme and is
the very substance of the controversy before us. Imagine
someone assuming the moral acceptability of bestiality.
The argument is precisely parallel to this one offered for
homosexuality. The argument would contend for the
acceptability of bestiality because it would not be practiced
in a "religious" manner, and every time bestiality is

mentioned in the Bible, it is prohibited in a context of religious, idolatrous practices (as it is in Exodus 22:19–20 and Deuteronomy 27:15–21). The problem with this line of argumentation is obvious: it assumes the moral acceptability of bestiality and would declare it to be immoral only when it is performed "religiously," thus making it idolatrous and, therefore, sinful.

Let us take the same approach with the sacrificing of children. Is this *ever* acceptable? Most of the biblical references to the sacrificing of children are connected with false, idolatrous worship. What is the moral conclusion that is to be drawn when we remove Molech, or any other false deity, from the situation of child sacrifice? If someone were to murder his children for the sake of convenience—doing so in a non-religious way, that is, not in a temple—would the practice be morally acceptable? Can any moral approval be gained when we restrict the practice of child sacrifice to a non-religious type (Deuteronomy 28:54–55; 1 Kings 3:26; 2 Kings 6:25–31; Matthew 2:16)? Certainly not! This obvious point further illustrates the shaky position of those who are contending that the Leviticus passages refer only to the pagan religious exercise of homosexual prostitution: they are assuming the moral acceptability of that which they are trying to prove.

One more example: Dr. Pearson's citation of Scripture is rather selective. He cited Leviticus 18:21–24, mentioning that "all four verses must be taken together." Why did he stop at these four verses? Why did he exclude verse 20 of chapter 18? Interestingly, Leviticus 18:20 refers to adultery, and if Pearson's contention is correct, that this is a context of "temple cult prostitution," adultery would obviously be in view as well. Surely Pearson knows, however, that such a slope is slippery and dangerous to navigate. Adultery, as with child sacrifice, bestiality, and homosexuality, is not acceptable if one merely removes the religious prostitution aspect. Adultery is prohibited in the temple (Hophni and Phineas, for example, in 1 Samuel 2:22) and in the town (David with Bathsheba, 2 Samuel 11).

For all persons everywhere, not just the people that follow the God of Abraham, Isaac, and Jacob, adultery is wrong because it is a violation of God's moral law as articulated in the Seventh Commandment. Just as it is wrong for those who are following the God of the Bible, so too it is wrong for those "outside of Israel." Dr. Greg Bahnsen is correct in his comment: "The Bible condemns the sex life of the heathen town as well as the sexual idolatry of the heathen temple."[5] Adultery is prohibited whether it is practiced in private or in public, in a chamber or in a temple. Pearson's citation of Leviticus 18 is selective; consistency is too revealing for the revisionist position. It is obvious that those who are trying to re-work the context of Leviticus to fit their sexual preferences stand guilty before the very same passages.

This particular approach to evading the Leviticus prohibitions actually becomes a bit more complicated when those who espouse it also cite the Hebrew language in support of their agenda. They are correct in pointing out that the word translated "sodomite" (KJV) or "male cult prostitute" (NASB) in 1 Kings 14:24; 15:12; 22:46; and 2 Kings 23:7 is the word *qadesh* and refers to something, or someone, who is consecrated, set apart for special (dedicated) service. These persons were religiously committed prostitutes, practicing their craft in the name of their faith.

Persons on both sides of this same-sex controversy are generally agreed that these persons in First and Second Kings are homosexual temple prostitutes who are designated by the term *qadesh*; however, this work with the word *qadesh* does nothing to prove that the homosexual behavior referred to in Leviticus chapters 18 and 20 is homosexual temple prostitution. The word *qadesh* is not even used in Leviticus 18:22 or 20:13. This fact is significant because the word *qadesh* was known and used by Moses in the Pentateuch in Deuteronomy 23:17: "None of the daughters of Israel shall be a cult prostitute (*qadesh*), nor shall any of the sons of Israel be a cult prostitute (*qadesh*)." Moses could have used the word in Leviticus; it was known by him and available, yet he did not use it.

Finally, the attempt to reconstruct the biblical backgrounds to fit into the mold of a false understanding of the Leviticus passages fails when one considers the descriptive phraseology employed by Moses. He did not use a single word or term to refer to the homosexuality. Rather, he *describes* the behavior as those "who lie with [so as to go to bed with] a male as one lies with [so as to go to bed with] a female" (18:22). The word that is used to describe this "lying with" in Leviticus 18:22 and 20:13 is the very same Hebrew word that is used for a bed and for sexual intercourse.[6] The word refers to male intercourse. The Leviticus passages are not unclear; they are very clear and stand convincingly relevant in our present day.

Leviticus and Lesbianism

The charge that Leviticus may condemn male-male sexual intimacy but does not condemn female-female sexual intimacy (lesbianism) is not uncommon. Scanzoni and Mollenkott remark, "It should be noticed that female homosexuality is not mentioned in the Holiness Code, even though women were certainly not ignored in the other sexual behaviors mentioned therein."[7]

While we cannot answer every objection that is brought up by those who claim that the Bible supports their homosexual practices (or at least does not forbid them), this one we must answer as it is gaining in popularity in the absence of biblical thinking in our day.

First of all, absence of a direct comment in Holy Scripture does not render a behavior morally acceptable. Similarly, a distinct prohibition in the pages of Holy Scripture is not needed to render some behavior morally reprehensible. For example, the Bible nowhere condemns necrophilia, and yet this fact does not make the practice morally acceptable. We have already noted that the Bible nowhere *with one specific Bible verse* condemns pedophilia with those who are outside of one's own family. Absence of such a verse surely does not make the practice right.

Take, for example, Leviticus 18, where we read of the prohibition of "uncovering the nakedness" of any blood relative. These are holy prohibitions with regard to incest. Striking in its absence is *any specific reference to a man's flesh-and-blood daughter.* Now, we would grant that incest with one's own daughter is prohibited in verse 6: "None of you shall approach any blood relative of his to uncover his nakedness; I am the LORD." In this section of Scripture, Moses makes no specific reference to one's own daughter, even though he goes on to list various other relationships that could be in view. Also absent is any reference to uncovering the nakedness of an adopted child. If the case is going to be made that lesbianism is an acceptable practice because it is not specifically referenced, then a whole host of other problems will also come to the surface of this immoral well.

Second, with those who bring up this "no reference to lesbianism" objection, we often hear the Bible being decried as sexist because it is predominately male-oriented. Now, this view is fascinating in that the very persons who claim that the Bible has nothing to say about female-female homosexuality also recognize that the Bible is speaking in a patriarchal manner. They seem oblivious to the fact that this realization supports the view that the prohibition against male-male sexual intimacy is also a prohibition against female-female sexual intimacy.

So the prohibition against same-sex intimacy found in Leviticus, while referring to men, would also include women under its ban, and this understanding is wholly consistent with other passages in the Bible. Since the entire Bible is authoritative from cover to cover, we are not surprised to find the Leviticus prohibitions upheld in the New Testament. The apostle Paul in the book of Romans refers to the practice of lesbianism as that which evidences a life that has been "given over" by God in judgment (Romans 1:26–27).

Notes

1. *Dirt, Greed, and Sex*, 33. John Boswell, in *Christianity, Social Tolerance, and Homosexuality*, suggests this idea as well. See pages 100, 102.
2. *Is the Homosexual My Neighbor*, 59–60.
3. "Charlie Coppinger's Side of the 'Gay Chaplain' Story." *Active Christian News*, Dec. 2000: 7. It must be noted that Coppinger has butchered the word *monogamous*. The word is derived from a Greek word, *gamos*, which means marriage. Biblically speaking, a marriage *cannot* occur between members of the same sex (see chapter 8 of this book).
4. Dr. Joseph A. Pearson, *Christianity and Homosexuality (Reconciled)*, videotape, part 3.
5. *Homosexuality: A Biblical View*, 45.
6. The Hebrew word is *mish-cov* and, since it refers to both a *bed* (Exodus 8:3; 2 Samuel 4:7; 11:2) and to *intercourse* (Numbers 31:17–18, 35; Judges 21:11–12), this word is equivalent to our English slang of "going to bed with" or "sleeping with" another. This word, being used in Leviticus 18:22 and 20:13, clearly refers to male intercourse.
7. *Is the Homosexual My Neighbor*, 61.

CHAPTER SIX

Unnatural Affections, Unnatural Interpretation: Romans 1

For this reason God gave them over to degrading passions; for their women exchanged the natural function for that which is unnatural, and in the same way also the men abandoned the natural function of the woman and burned in their desire toward one another, men with men committing indecent acts and receiving in their own persons the due penalty of their error. (Romans 1:26–27)

Few sections of Scripture are more profound, more foundational to Christian thought, than the opening verses of Paul's epistle to the Romans. The first chapter has provided Christian writers with insights into the human condition that have resulted in some of the most important published works on the Christian worldview.

Western culture's view of law and ethics has been deeply influenced by these thirty-two verses. So it is hardly surprising that those who seek to undermine that Christian worldview and foundation invest great effort in reinterpreting these words, at least until they can be safely and openly dismissed as the irrelevant words many today already believe them to be.

In the debate between those who present a biblical view of human sexuality and those who seek to replace that view with one derived from modern philosophy and a humanistic worldview, Romans 1 takes center stage, and necessarily so. Of all biblical texts in this debate it is the most familiar and the most commonly cited. For many, its meaning is so transparent that it closes the door on any other sexual preference possibilities. Yet we must observe closely its structure and consistency, for the human mind has a tremendous capacity for finding ways around even the most obvious statements of truth.

ROMANS 1: MAN IN SIN

Before Paul can proclaim the good news of redemption in Jesus Christ, he must establish the *need* of that redemption. So the beginning of the letter that epitomizes the *good news* begins with two and a half chapters of *bad news*. These initial chapters of Romans provide an unquestionable demonstration of the sinfulness of man.

It is in the context of this necessary presentation of

man's need that we find the key texts that come into play in the debate over homosexuality. But it should be emphasized that these verses do not exist in a vacuum. They cannot be separated out and considered without realizing that they are a part of an entire presentation. And this presentation is one that confirms, beyond question, the essential correctness of the view Christians have held from the beginning: that Paul singles out homosexuality in Romans 1:26–27 as an illustration of the judgment of God upon those who refuse to acknowledge His lordship over their lives.

To establish the unquestionable nature of the argument, we must begin where Paul begins. Upon announcing the topic of his letter, the gospel (Romans 1:16–17), he turns immediately to the subject of *why* the gospel is so vital. Romans 1:18 reads,

> For the wrath of God is revealed from heaven against all ungodliness and unrighteousness of men, who suppress the truth in unrighteousness.

Men need deliverance from the wrath of God. This wrath is being revealed from heaven in an ongoing fashion, not merely against gross sin and immorality, but against "all ungodliness and unrighteousness of men." As God is holy, His wrath comes upon everything that is *not* holy, *all* ungodliness and unrighteousness.

The depth of man's sin is only increased by the description Paul gives of man's culpability. Man is not the ignorant innocent who should not be held accountable or who can offer an excuse. No, man *suppresses* the truth. The term is rich, in that we cannot suppress something that we do not already possess. Men are involved in suppressing the truth in unrighteousness. It should be emphasized that man's relationship to truth is not a neutral or "secondary" issue. To suppress the truth is a wicked act; it is an act of rebellion against one's Creator. Despite the popularity of the view in Western culture today, it is not a biblical belief to view truth as a neutral, non-moral issue. The suppression of truth is sinful. Giving positive assent to error *as an act of suppression* is sinful as well. This truth is rarely understood—oftentimes even this is suppressed.

Paul explains the basis of his assertion when he writes, "Because that which is known about God is evident within them; for God made it evident to them" (Romans 1:19). God's wrath is just and holy, for it comes upon those who have no excuse. God has actively revealed himself to those who are busily doing all they can to suppress that knowledge: "That which is known about God is evident within them." Some see this as referring to "within each individual" as one who is created by God, and therefore unable to escape God's revelation in our own person, while others see this as referring to within "them" as a group, i.e., within creation and society as a whole. Both are true as Paul goes on to explain:

> [20]For since the creation of the world His invisible attributes, His eternal power and divine nature, have been clearly seen, being understood through what has been made, so that they are without excuse.

Two vital elements of God's existence have been clearly revealed through creation itself: His eternal power and His divine nature. While this is surely not an exhaustive revelation of all there is to know about God (such is found solely in Christ, who is the "exact representation" of the Father's nature, Hebrews 1:3), it is sufficient to hold all mankind accountable, rendering humanity "without excuse," or more literally, "without a defense." The clarity of the revelation of the existence of the divine and powerful God who has made us brushes all excuses of ignorance aside. Man knows, but man suppresses. He knows he is accountable to God, and owes to God a debt of honor and gratitude for life itself, but he refuses to give it. Paul continues,

> [21]For even though they knew God, they did not honor Him as God or give thanks; but they became futile in their speculations, and their foolish heart was darkened. [22]Professing to be wise, they became fools, [23]and exchanged the glory of the incorruptible God for an image in the form of corruptible man and of birds and four-footed animals and crawling creatures.

Suppression is displayed in the form of *twisting*, as man, knowing he should honor the God who made him and give thanks for the many blessings he provides, substitutes futile, foolish speculations in the place of the knowledge of God. This results in a "twistedness" that marks all of human experience. They profess wisdom, but, since fear of the Lord is the beginning of wisdom (Proverbs

9:10), they are, in reality, fools. This perversity (claiming what one does not possess, namely, wisdom) leads to the twisting of man himself. The first element of this twisting is *religious* in nature. It is natural for man to worship. But when man rebels and refuses to give that worship to the only one worthy of it, God the Creator, he does not cease to worship. Instead, man engages in idolatry, the giving of that which rightfully and solely belongs to God to *anything* in the created order. For while those who worship in spirit and truth revel in the glory of their God, those who refuse to give Him His due honor are left "exchanging" that glory for a cheap imitation, mere images of the creation itself and not the Creator. The exchange is a poor one, of course. Only a twisted person who is seeking to suppress the knowledge of God would make it. And yet, that is what man does.

We should emphasize the fact that idolatry does not require one to bow down before a hideous idol in the dark recesses of the earth. Idolatry expresses itself in many ways. The person who idolizes science, technology, or human philosophy is engaging in idolatry. The persons giving their time and energy to fulfilling their own selfish lusts engage in idolatry as well. Idolatry speaks to the entirety of man's activities wherein he seeks to express his natural urge to worship outside of the parameters God has established (Colossians 3:5).

> [24]Therefore God gave them over in the lusts of their hearts to impurity, so that their bodies would be dishon-

ored among them. [25]For they exchanged the truth of God for a lie, and worshiped and served the creature rather than the Creator, who is blessed forever. Amen.

Verse 24 introduces the result of man's twisted refusal to honor God and the resultant descent into idolatry: God "gives them over."[1] This is a judicial act on God's part. In essence He says, "If what you wish is to wallow in your sin, then your punishment will be to do just that, for your sin will consume you." The cycle of sin is vicious, and outside of grace, unending. What was once an attraction becomes a degrading addiction. The man and woman caught in the trap of sin are dishonored by their servitude to its power. And while the attitudes described so far have existed primarily in the mind (suppression, idolatry), man is a single unit. The mind that dwells upon dishonorable thoughts will result in a body that is dishonored in the actions that flow from such a mindset. People who rebel against God eventually find themselves freed to revel in their rebellion, to their demise.

Verse 25 reminds us of what brings this kind of judgment from God. The theme of twisting and exchange is repeated. These people have exchanged what they possessed naturally—the truth of God (v. 20)—for a lie, or more literally, for *the* lie. This is a "deal" they desperately want, for the truth of God tortures their conscience, and they will seek any kind of remedy to silence its voice. Though man was not made to tell, or embrace, untruth, in his rebellion he sets his affections upon what is unnatural: a lie. And while he knows it is a lie, he prefers the lie to the truth that brings conviction of his rebellion and sin. He works to convince himself he loves this lie, and in time, he is successful.

The worship and service of man's soul, that insatiable religious nature of the creature made in God's image, cannot avoid the twisting that sin brings. As we already noted, man will worship, but when he is actively involved in suppressing the truth about God, that worship will be focused anywhere but upon the true and living God. And so that which is created worships and serves that which is likewise created, all in the effort to avoid recognizing the blessed Creator. The twistedness becomes blatant and increasingly reprehensible.

This then provides the context to the two key verses:

> [26]For this reason God gave them over to degrading passions; for their women exchanged the natural function for that which is unnatural, [27]and in the same way also the men abandoned the natural function of the woman and burned in their desire toward one another, men with men committing indecent acts and receiving in their own persons the due penalty of their error.

These verses form a single sentence, connected directly to the preceding words by "for this reason." Paul does not depart from his theme at this point. These verses are not some separated, a-contextual leap into another subject. The theme continues without a break. But here Paul teaches that because of the idolatry of mankind God gives men over to "degrading passions" (NASB), "shameful lusts" (NIV), "vile passions" (NKJV). However the phrase is translated, it obviously refers to desires and passions that are dishonorable and indicative of God's judgment upon those who indulge in selfish, lustful behavior.

Paul then gives a fitting example of these "degrading passions," one that illustrates "twistedness" at the very core of human identity. He first mentions lesbianism, describing, clearly, adult, mutual lesbian activity. This is seen in the description given in both verses 26 and 27, for verse 27 begins with "and in the same way," indicating that the description of male homosexual activity in that verse is parallel to the lesbian activity in verse 26. Hence, the description of lesbianism as "against nature" in verse 26 would apply to male homosexuality as well, and the description of mutuality and "indecent acts" in verse 27 would apply to lesbian activity as well.

There is a note of sadness in Paul's words, "for *even* their women . . ." (NIV and NKJV). The female, as a result of the twistedness of sin, exchanges the "natural sexual function" (the most basic meaning of the words Paul uses) for that which is "against nature." This is a voluntary act. These women *exchange* the natural function for that which is against nature. There is choice involved here, a choice that expresses the twistedness of the rebellion against the Creator that Paul is illustrating. The "natural sexual function" is still known to these women, but they *choose* to "exchange" it. Paul uses the very same term he had used in the preceding verse, "*exchanging* the truth of

God for the lie," so obviously this exchange carries the same negative character: the exchange of God's truth for a lie is the same as exchanging the natural sexual use for the unnatural. The choice is purposeful in the first, and it is in the second as well.

The meaning of "against nature" is defined by the context. The word translated "sexual function" is not ambiguous or questionable. The conjunction of the word for "natural" is likewise clear, and the resulting phrase "natural sexual function" is easily understood both by Paul's original audience and by any unbiased person today. He is referring to the way God created human beings, male and female, and the sexual union that takes place between a man and a woman. This is what has been "exchanged" in the downward spiral of sinfulness. God created women with a natural sexual function. When one rebels against God's truth and exchanges it for a lie, that lie impacts everything else in one's life. The natural function is exchanged for that which is against nature, that is, unnatural, against the created order.

Verse 27 is a continuation of the same thought. It begins "in the same way," tying the two verses together without question. Verse 26 spoke of "the women," and verse 27 begins "the men." The men "abandoned" or "left" the "natural use" of the woman. Paul uses the same words here he used of lesbianism: these men have abandoned (another word signifying choice) the *natural sexual use* of the woman ("natural relations," NIV). God's intention in the sexual expression of His creatures is to be between a man and a woman, just as it was with Adam and Eve. This is the natural sexual function. But these men abandon this. They know what it is, but they reject it, they "leave" it.

Paul's description of homosexuality is clear and without compromise. "They burned in their desire toward one another" (NASB) is rendered by the NIV, "were inflamed with lust for one another." Both terms speak clearly of sexual lust and desire. These desires are consuming. Such would point us toward an ongoing lifestyle, not a single incident of sexual debauchery. And these desires are mutual. The desire goes both ways, one homosexual man desiring another, and vice-versa. This point is important to remember in reference to revisionist attempts to blunt the force of this passage.

The mutuality of this desire is emphasized by the phrase "men with men." The apostle leaves no doubt as to his reference: adult homosexuals. And these are *active* men: They act upon their desires, accomplishing what Paul identifies as literally "the shameful deed," or as it is rendered by the NASB and NIV, "indecent acts." The term comes from an old word that referred to something as "deformed," and hence flows into the concept of perversion and deviation that is part and parcel of this section of the chapter. There is no possible way of reading this term as referring to anything neutral or simply "unusual" or "out of the norm." Paul views homosexual activity as shameful or indecent.

This fact is further proven by the final phrase of verse

27. He writes, "and receiving in their own persons the due penalty of their error." Man cannot expect to engage in deviant activity without receiving the "due penalty." While interpreters differ over the extent and meaning of the "penalty" and how it is received "in their own persons," a number of facts are beyond question. First, the fact that a "penalty" or "punishment" is attached to the "error" of performing these "shameful deeds" reinforces the understanding that these are sinful deeds, worthy of retribution. Second, this is a "due" or "necessary" punishment; it is fitting that such deeds receive a penalty: God's justice demands that the twisting of His created order receive a punitive response. Third, their "error" is not merely a "miscalculation" as we might use the term "error" today. Indeed, a better rendering of this term, which often is used in the New Testament to refer to being misled or drawn from the right path, is "perversion," just as the NIV renders it, "the due penalty for their perversion."

Again, opinions differ as to what receiving the penalty due to their error "in their own persons" means. Some believe, along with John Chrysostom, one of the leading commentators of the early Christian church, that the penalty referred to in this passage is the sexual perversion itself. It becomes a cycle, the sin degrading the sinner who is trapped by his or her own lusts. Others believe this to refer to their final punishment, which they will receive "in their own persons"—the penalty due their blatant violation of God's will. Of course, with the spread of the AIDS epidemic, many have attempted to connect this passage with the disease. AIDS, however, impacts non-homosexual offenders as well, and not *every* homosexual offender receives this punishment. From Paul's perspective, whatever this punishment is, *all* those who engage in this behavior receive the due penalty for their perversion.

Since we do not have an utterance from God as to a one-to-one correspondence between homosexual behavior and AIDS, we must be careful about making definitive assertions about their correlation. However, we can assuredly declare that all sin, since it is destructive to individuals and societies, does deserve—and often receives—frightful and deadly penalties; God does judge sinners, He reveals His wrath against all ungodliness and unrighteousness. The fact that some non-homosexuals have AIDS does nothing to overturn the fact of God's holy wrath being exercised against all ungodliness and unrighteousness. Sin, especially that of a public nature, affects others, and often the penalty affects others too. . . . Jeremiah, for instance, was swept away in Babylonian captivity.

The next verses continue on without any hint of a break or discontinuity of thought. In fact, the theme of judicial "giving over" of rebel sinners continues uninterrupted as well. And while the length of the passage obscures this fact, we have here a single sentence, and the final thought is connected directly to everything that came before, *including* 1:26–27:

> [28]And just as they did not see fit to acknowledge God any longer, God gave them over to a depraved mind, to

do those things which are not proper, [29]being filled with all unrighteousness, wickedness, greed, evil; full of envy, murder, strife, deceit, malice; they are gossips, [30]slanderers, haters of God, insolent, arrogant, boastful, inventors of evil, disobedient to parents, [31]without understanding, untrustworthy, unloving, unmerciful; [32]and although they know the ordinance of God, that those who practice such things are worthy of death, they not only do the same, but also give hearty approval to those who practice them.

Verse 28 repeats the idea of judgment coming upon those who are involved in that suppression of knowledge with which Paul began his discussion (1:18). Before he described the result of this suppression as foolishness and darkness. Now he says that God gives men over to a "depraved mind," resulting in the catalog of sins that comes in verses 29 through 31. Though created in the image of God, the very crowning jewel of creation itself, man is so twisted as to rebel against His Maker, banish fear of God from his mind, and engage in behavior that he *knows* is contrary to the law of the One who formed and made him.

Verse 32 is not only a summary of the preceding clauses of the single sentence that makes up 1:28–32, but of the entire section. Sin has so twisted the mind of man that even when he *knows* full well the result of his actions, he not only willfully chooses to continue in them but is also active in encouraging the very same insanity among his fellow creatures! The guilty man on death row, fully knowing his condemnation, often continues in his life of crime and tries to get as many as he can to join him! How consistent is man in sin: from suppression of truth to the final result of self-destruction in the face of certain judgment. The one created in the image of God, knowing full well the righteousness of God's condemnation of sin, rushes blindly on, striving to drag as many as possible with him. In this passage of Scripture we see twistedness in the harshest light of reality.

Thus we see the plain teaching of the apostle. These words have been understood to express God's disapproval of all of the aforementioned sins and transgressions, *including homosexuality,* down through the centuries since the founding of the Christian church. And yet today many seek to deflect the weight of these words in the most novel ways. We now turn to the vindication of the text (for surely, given the clarity of the passage, any revision of its teaching requires a fundamental attack upon it as well) and the refutation of the attempts of revisionists to remove this passage from the body of revelation that should guide our understanding of God's will for our lives.

A Note Concerning the Plethora of Objections

The number of objections and attempts to redefine the words of the apostle in Romans 1 is large indeed. A few comments are necessary before examining these attempts.

First, many books utilize the "Ph.D." method of obfuscation at this point: **P**iled **h**igher and **D**eeper. Seemingly, the author—or authors—of such revisions believes it best to multiply possible scenarios as to Paul's meaning in this passage, perhaps hopeful of presenting the idea that there are many possible ways to answer the traditional objections to homosexuality. Many of the less scholarly revisionists' works (those that do not present a single focused attempt to redefine Paul's meaning) will multiply possible understandings, seemingly in the hope of so muddling the thinking of the readers that they will throw up their hands in despair and assume that no one can really know what Paul was talking about since so many "scholars" are "confused" as to the real meaning of the passage. At times the views cited within a single work can be seen to be self-contradictory, but this passes without even a notation. This only adds to the confusion.

At other times, when a scholar presents a specific interpretation, that view may well be directly contradictory to the conclusions of another pro-homosexual author or scholar. The pro-homosexual, revisionist literature hardly presents a single coherent whole when it comes to its methods of "exegesis" and the conclusions it comes to. But there is one consistency in all the revisionist literature: an absolute refusal to allow for the possibility that the historical Christian viewpoint on the matter is correct. No matter what other conclusions are reached, the one that *cannot* be true is the one Christians have proclaimed from the beginning. This consideration alone is very telling.

Objection Stated

What is "natural" in Romans 1 is not what is "natural" in the sense of "natural law," but what is "natural to me." The reference is not to homosexuals but to heterosexuals who go beyond their natural bounds and engage in homosexuality.

Thus John Boswell writes,

On the other hand, it should be recognized that the point of the passage is not to stigmatize sexual behavior of any sort but to condemn the Gentiles for their general infidelity. . . . The reference to homosexuality is simply a mundane analogy to this theological sin; it is patently not the crux of this argument. . . . What is even more important, the persons Paul condemns are manifestly not homosexual: what he derogates are homosexual acts committed by apparently heterosexual persons. The whole point of Romans 1, in fact, is to stigmatize persons who have rejected their calling, gotten off the true path they were once on. It would completely undermine the thrust of the argument if the persons in question were not "naturally" inclined to the opposite sex in the same way they were "naturally" inclined to monotheism.[2]

Biblical Response

This perspective, presented in some of the most popular revisionist works,[3] tries to find a way to allow for a "natural" homosexuality by reading *out* of the text the basic meaning. Our exegesis has already shown, however, that this viewpoint is untenable. The entire context would be completely disrupted by such an eisegetical[4] reading. The focus upon the willful *twisting* of God's truth, and the resultant judicial "giving over" of men to the results of their own refusal to worship Him and acknowledge Him, is utterly lost if, in fact, the only point here is that homosexuality itself is not sinful in God's sight, but rather it is wrong to engage in it if you have "natural" desires.

The above quote from John Boswell contains numerous errors. Aside from the impossible task of understanding what "general infidelity" can possibly mean, it is surely untrue that Romans 1:26–27 "is simply a mundane analogy." Such is a complete misreading of the flow of the text that we established above.

Next, it is very instructive to read a scholar stating, "The persons Paul condemns are manifestly not homosexual." Remember that this passage specifically speaks of adult men who engage in mutual sexual desire and activity. It is eisegesis in the extreme to dismiss this clear description of basic homosexual activity on the basis of the extra-contextual assertion that since these men *chose* this activity then it must follow that they were not "true" homosexuals. The hidden, and false, assumption is that homosexuals do not *choose* to engage in the activities they do. Homosexuals "are the way they are" and did not, and *do not*, choose to do what they do. But such is obviously far from the apostle's meaning, let alone the truth. The words of Romans 1 would apply to anyone engaging in homosexual activities or desires, and this is exactly what we see in the modern homosexual movement. To attempt to insert an anachronistic definition into the text so as to exclude the very audience of the descriptions given by Paul is the height of eisegesis. Nor does it touch the heart of Paul's assertion: that the twisting of God's creative design in man and woman is exemplary of the pervasiveness of man's desire to replace the true knowledge of God with "the lie."

To adopt Boswell's position is to turn Paul's argument on its head, for his opponents could easily retort, "Well, that is only true in a certain group, but other than those, the 'natural' homosexual activity of 'true' homosexuals who likewise desire one another would not show this 'twistedness' you are attempting to demonstrate."

Paul's argument does not allow this shift in meaning. The meaning of the words (the "natural use" of the male or female, the active choice to engage in homosexual behavior, the desire expressed in the mutuality of the activity) and the context of the argument (God has given them over to "degrading passions," and they remain degrading no matter who is engaging in them) militate strongly against this revisionist attempt.

Objection Stated

Paul did not know about "inversion" and mutuality, and hence this passage does not have relevance today.

Biblical Response

There are two things to be noted in response to this assertion—an assertion that is, truly, at the bottom of almost every argument on the part of revisionists. The first is the unspoken, but foundational, assumption that the Scriptures are limited in their capacity and hence authority to the knowledge and experience of the human authors by which they were delivered to us. The second is more overt: Paul did not know about "inversion" or the allegedly "natural" occurrence of homosexuality. Let's begin with the second objection.

Paul came from Tarsus, a major city in the Roman empire. He was well trained, a learned man, familiar with Roman and Greek culture. He was obviously widely read in the literature of the day as well. Therefore, the assumption that he did not know of people who professed to be homosexual as their primary "orientation" is simply far-fetched unless one is willing to say that in essence no one really "knew" about this until the past few decades or centuries. Further, it is self-evident that the full outline of the modern homosexual view of orientation *was* known in the ancient world, despite the oft-repeated assertion that it was not. Plato's *Symposium*, written centuries before Paul wrote Romans, showed that the ancients were well aware of all the elements of modern homosexual behavior, even if they did not use the same exact words. Plato's writings make reference to male homosexuality, lesbianism, the claims of some to be born as a willing mate of a man, the concept of mutuality, permanency, gay pride, pederasty, "homophobia," motive, desire, passion, etc.[5] One would have to assume Paul a very poor student *and* a very poor observer of the culture around him to be unaware of these things.

The second objection will be dealt with fully in chapter 8, but should be given some mention here as well. At the base of all revisionist arguments is a less-than-robust, and at times, simply non-existent, doctrine of Scripture. If the Bible is in fact *theopneustos*, "God-breathed," as Paul insists (2 Timothy 3:16), then the question that must be asked is, "Does God's wisdom and knowledge allow Him to clearly reveal His truth to His people despite any and all limitations of knowledge on the part of those He chooses to be His instruments in the recording of His Word?" Indeed, one may well ask if God could not choose someone to be used in this fashion who would *not* be ignorant of the very things that God wishes to address, such as the debauchery and idolatry of those who suppress the knowledge of God that is within them. Surely an omnipotent God who desires to communicate himself clearly is capable of accomplishing His task. Christians have always believed He fulfilled His desire in the inspiration of the Scriptures, and that they therefore can function as an infallible and sufficient rule of faith and obedience for God's people. Revisionists, seeking a way around the clear revelation of God's will in those Scriptures, seek to ameliorate the pressure brought to bear upon either their lifestyle or their unorthodox beliefs by undercutting the authority of the Word by muting the clarity of its voice.

Objection Stated

Paul is only speaking of pederasty here, not of adult homosexual relationships, and hence the passage is misused when applied to homosexuality.

This is the viewpoint expressed by Robin Scroggs in his work *The New Testament and Homosexuality*.[6] It is commonly repeated in liberal theological institutions.

Biblical Response

The exegesis of the passage has already addressed this common error. Paul speaks of "males with males committing indecent acts." He does not say "men with boys" (and there are appropriate Greek words that Paul could have employed if he meant to communicate this idea), nor does the text give the slightest hint that this should be read into it as an assumption. The desire expressed is mutual between both the lesbians of 1:26 and the homosexual males of 1:27; that is, there is no evidence whatsoever that this is written in reference to pederastic relationships. Indeed, the mutual kind of desire seen in these verses utterly refutes the simplistic assertion that these words are to be limited to pederasty.

Scroggs and others claim the language is a stereotypical "Greco-Roman attack on pederasty" and that "it has nothing to do with any theories of natural law or with interpretation of the Genesis stories of creation."[7] But we have seen that rather than drawing from some stereotypical language here, Paul's point flows naturally through the entire discourse. He most assuredly *is* drawing from Genesis and God's creative decree, as he does so often in his writings.

Objection Stated

Paul is speaking solely of Jewish purity laws, and hence this is irrelevant in a modern, enlightened society.

Biblical Response

It needs to be acknowledged from the outset, and this illustrates the constant inconsistency found among the revisionist interpreters, that this is an admission that the Hebrew Scriptures do indeed condemn homosexual deeds and desires. After all, if Paul's condemnation of such sinfulness is drawn from Judaism, this is a tacit admission that Judaism opposed homosexuality. We have addressed the basic contention of the allegedly limited application of God's moral laws in our discussion of the

Leviticus passages. It seems sufficient at this point to note how such an objection completely misses Paul's context as well as his argument.

Paul surely did not embrace modern views of either God's law or God's revelation in the Jewish Scriptures. He would not have held to the concept that the revelation of God's holy will in Scripture was somehow to be limited "only to the Jews" nor would he have seen God's moral pronouncements to be relics of a "holiness code." It is obvious that for Paul and the other apostles the repeated proclamation of God's role as Creator of the world and of mankind, found throughout the Scriptures, meant that God's revelation of His law was as universal as the truth that He is the Creator. All men are created in the image of God, and all men bear that unmistakable imprint of "creature" upon their soul. To limit the Levitical prohibitions against homosexuality to Israel alone, or to a particular period, or a particular geographical location, assumes a view of God and His law that Paul surely did not embrace.

Further, such an objection is without merit in this context, as it would force us to believe that Paul is not consistent in his own argumentation. Paul has spoken in broad, creation-wide terms from verse 18 onward. He has spoken in universal terms of man's refusal to acknowledge God, his Creator, and the resultant actions of man attendant to the suppression of the truth that exists all around him, and from which there is no escape. Again, no limitation to merely Jewish "purity codes" is found up to this point.

Then Paul speaks of God's judicial giving over of men and women to the dominion of the sins they hold so dear, and the resulting "twistedness" of their relationship to God, the world around them, and to themselves. These words apply far beyond the boundaries of Jewish purity laws. They speak to the revelation of God's will for mankind, not merely for Jews. The expanse and breadth of His words cannot be dismissed by such a cavalier explanation.

Objection Stated

Paul does not identify homosexuality, which is indeed mentioned in Romans 1:26–27, as sin.

This seems to be the thrust of L. William Countryman when he writes, "The idea that Paul was labeling homosexual acts as sinful can be upheld only if one can show that he used other terms here with an equivalent meaning."[8] And in a public debate, this was ACLU board member and head of Americans United for the Separation of Church and State Barry Lynn's common refrain when dealing with Romans 1, that Paul specifically avoided saying homosexuality was a sin.[9]

Biblical Response

This revisionist attempt is surely one of the weakest offered, for it requires us to believe all of the following propositions: first, that in the midst of demonstrating the awful sinfulness of idolatry and its punishment, Paul would insert a sentence where he switches subjects to something that, while possibly "unusual" in a social sense, is not actually sinful; second, that the context is to be broken up with no connection seen (despite the summary statement of 1:32); and finally, that when Paul spoke of "degrading passions," "indecent acts," and how those committing them would receive the "due penalty of their error," these are not indications of sinfulness. The mere repetition of the assertions in light of the exegesis of the text already provided is sufficient refutation.

Objection Stated

Paul is not giving a binding, for-all-time concept here, but is speaking only about what was then "natural" in a conventional or social sense.

Biblical Response

The basis of Paul's discussion in Romans 1, aside from establishing the very foundation upon which he intends to present the gospel for all people (and, it can be argued, for all time), gives us no hint that the author intends his words to be limited geographically or temporally. The concepts he presents reach back to creation itself, apply over and beyond all cultural boundaries, and speak to men and women at the very level of their existence, not merely in their cultural climate. It is to completely remove the passage from its original context and purpose to say that it merely speaks to what is "unusual" and hence to be avoided for the mere sake of appearance. Human convention or social morality is not in Paul's thinking here, for he grounds his words in God's creative purpose and decree. This argument is really based upon the assertion that Scripture not so much *does not* as *cannot* give binding, eternal, extra-cultural norms of behavior, truth, and morality.

Objection Stated

Paul is "trapping" the Jews in Romans 1, and springs the trap in Romans 2, and hence what is in Romans 1 is really irrelevant to the modern situation.

Some revisionists argue that Paul's entire effort in Romans 1 is in essence disingenuous: He is simply seeking to get his Jewish opponents to agree with him, to "jump on the bandwagon" so to speak, so he can then "spring the trap" on them in chapter two. The hoped for result seems to be that we can dismiss what Paul says in chapter 1 as merely rhetorical.

Biblical Response

This kind of argument can be very fairly identified as desperate. The consistency of what Paul says in Romans 1 and how he concludes Romans 3 (vv. 10–19), which comes long after the alleged "springing of the trap" in chapter 2, completely refutes this idea. Further, the argument assumes that Paul is speaking *only* of Gentiles in chapter 1, which is simply untrue. The connection with chapter 2 and the direct application to Jews is not that Jews do not likewise sin in the fashion of those in chapter 1, but that they *refuse to acknowledge this* due to hypocrisy. There is simply no basis for rejecting the teaching of Romans 1 on the basis of such an objection.

Objection Stated

The sinners mentioned in Romans 1:26–27 are, in context, only idolaters who have taken specific and serious steps to deny the existence of God. Christian homosexuals do not take these steps, hence, the passage is not relevant to them.

Letha Scanzoni and Virginia Ramey Mollenkott likewise seem to have this kind of argument in mind when they write regarding Romans 1:

> The key thoughts seem to be lust, "unnaturalness," and, in verse 28, a desire to avoid acknowledgment of God. But although the censure fits the idolatrous people with whom Paul was concerned here, it does not fit the case of a sincere homosexual Christian. Such a person loves Jesus Christ and wants above all to acknowledge God in all of life, yet for some unknown reason feels drawn to someone of the same sex—*not* because of lust,

but because of sincere, heartfelt love. Is it fair to describe that person as lustful or desirous of forgetting God's existence?[10]

Biblical Response

This entire argument begs the question. It assumes a particular biblical conclusion with its insertion of the idea of "Christian homosexuals" right from the start and, having done so, uses its conclusion to reinterpret the Scriptures. The term "Christian homosexual" as it is being used by Scanzoni and Mollenkott in the above quotation is an oxymoron, just as using "Christian inventor of evil" (Romans 1:30) or "Christian who practices regular wickedness" (Romans 1:29) would violate all canons of logic and truth. Further, the argument makes idolatry a separate and distinct sin rather than seeing how it is related to everything the passage is addressing. Those who are suppressing the knowledge of God (a universal charge) express that rebellion in many ways, including homosexual behavior and all the other sinful activities listed in 1:28*ff.*

An advocate of homosexual behavior once presented this argument to the authors of this work on a radio program. He outlined what he called the "seven steps" of idolatry that had been mentioned in the previous verses, and proclaimed that since neither he, nor anyone in his congregation, had taken these seven steps, the passage had nothing to do with him. In response we pointed out that if, in fact, one had to undertake the various steps of attempting to deny God, etc., that he insisted one had to do *before* this passage was relevant, then it followed inevitably that all the other sins mentioned at the end of the chapter would likewise require one to engage first in the "seven steps" and then in those sins before they would truly *be* sins. But such is obviously not the apostle's intention. Such reasoning leads one to believe that it is okay to murder (1:29) as long as you have not sought to suppress the knowledge of God! Obviously, it is not the apostle's intention to limit his condemnation of the practice of lesbianism and homosexuality to a particular group of people who have first fulfilled a certain set of sinful attitudes and actions.

Notes

1. Throughout the Bible, God's judicial acts are often presented as His releasing—the giving over—of persons to the very sins in which they have indulged. See Psalm 28:4; 106:15; 109:17; Judges 1:7; Isaiah 3:10–11; Ezekiel 7:4, 27; 9:10; 2 Peter 2:10, 18–19 for examples of this. See appendix D, "Sin and the Penalty of Sin the Same," for Augustine's comments in this regard.

2. *Christianity, Social Tolerance, and Homosexuality*, 108–09.

3. Letha Scanzoni and Virginia Ramey Mollenkott, *Is the Homosexual My Neighbor?* present a bewildering array of "possibilities" in their discussion of Romans 1 (66–74), including, it seems, this one. As with so many revisionist works, the intention seems to be to present so many possibilities or theories that the reader is left with the distinct impression that *no one could possibly know* what the text is actually talking about, and any who say they do are obviously unaware of all these other "possibilities."

4. Eisegesis is the common error of "reading into" a text a meaning that the original author and context did not intend. It is the opposite of "exegesis," the proper interpretation of a text in its original context.

5. James B. DeYoung provides a full discussion of this very issue in his work *Homosexuality: Contemporary Claims Examined in the Light of the Bible and Other Ancient Literature and Law* (Grand Rapids: Kregel, 2000), Excursus Three, 205*ff.*

6. Robin Scroggs, *The New Testament and Homosexuality* (Minneapolis: Fortress Press, 1983), 109–18.

7. Ibid., 114–15.

8. *Dirt, Greed, and Sex*, 110.

9. James White vs. Barry Lynn, "Is Homosexuality Consistent With Biblical Christianity?" May 24, 2001, Huntington, Long Island.

10. *Is the Homosexual My Neighbor*, 67.

CHAPTER SEVEN

Desperately Defining Terms: 1 Corinthians and 1 Timothy

Or do you not know that the unrighteous shall not inherit the kingdom of God? Do not be deceived; neither fornicators, nor idolaters, nor adulterers, nor effeminate, nor homosexuals, nor thieves, nor the covetous, nor drunkards, nor revilers, nor swindlers, shall inherit the kingdom of God. (1 Corinthians 6:9–10)

But we know that the Law is good, if one uses it lawfully, realizing the fact that law is not made for a righteous man, but for those who are lawless and rebellious, for the ungodly and sinners, for the unholy and profane, for those who kill their fathers or mothers, for murderers and immoral men and homosexuals and kidnappers and liars and perjurers, and whatever else is contrary to sound teaching. (1 Timothy 1:8–10)

The apostle Paul wrote to a number of Christian congregations spread across the Roman empire. As he
addressed the many issues facing the primitive church, he
was bound to address the topic of morality, especially
when writing to those churches in cities known for their
promiscuity and debauchery. None was better known in
the ancient world than Corinth, so much so that the name
of the city was a synonym for sexual sin and immoral
behavior. The presence of centers of pagan religion associated directly with temple prostitution in the city led to
every kind of sexual license and activity.

The church at Corinth was plagued with many problems. Paul's correspondence to this particular congregation takes up the largest portion of his epistolary literature. The issues he was forced to address read like an
elder's nightmare list of congregational problems. Everything from doctrinal errors to internal strife to moral fail-
ures found a place in the laundry list of Corinthian
church ills. And it is in this context that we encounter a
reference to the topic of homosexuality.

Beginning in chapter five of Paul's first epistle to the
Corinthians we see that from the apostle's viewpoint, the
church at Corinth was to be held responsible to exercise
discipline in her ranks, a discipline that involved the application of the moral principles specifically laid out in the
Pentateuch. Paul cites directly from Deuteronomy 17:7 in
1 Corinthians 5:13, expecting his readers to fully understand the relevance of these words to their situation.

But especially relevant to Paul's discussion is the Holiness Code of Leviticus 18–20. We have already noted the frequency with which New Testament writers make reference to this section, including Jesus' citation of Leviticus 19:18 in Matthew 5:43; 19:19; 22:39; Mark 12:31; and Luke 10:27. Paul cites the same summary in Romans 13:9 and Galatians 5:14, and James quotes it in James 2:8. Paul's admonition to the Corinthians assumes the authoritative application of God's law (particularly this portion in Leviticus) and that the church in Corinth is familiar with this section of the law and, indeed, knows it is to be held accountable to living in light of its guidance. Paul is teaching the young believers at Corinth that they are to live lives of separation and holiness to God, just as the corresponding section in Leviticus gives guidance as to how Israel was to be distinct from the Gentile nations. Paul speaks of how the Christians should not be entrusting judgment to unbelievers when they themselves will exercise judgment (6:1–7). Judging assumes the existence of a standard of judgment, and Paul's allusions to the Mosaic standards within the very same section point us to the standard that was obviously in his mind. It is in this context that Paul writes,

> [9]Or do you not know that the unrighteous shall not inherit the kingdom of God? Do not be deceived; neither fornicators, nor idolaters, nor adulterers, nor effeminate, nor homosexuals, [10]nor thieves, nor the covetous, nor drunkards, nor revilers, nor swindlers, shall inherit the kingdom of God. [11]And such were some of you; but you were washed, but you were sanctified, but you were justified in the name of the LORD Jesus Christ and in the Spirit of our God.

The introductory phrase "do you not know" speaks of a given in Paul's thinking and teaching. Furthermore, he expects his audience to *already know* the truths he is about to reiterate. He has obviously already covered this ground with the Corinthians, and hence upbraids them for not clearly seeing the centrality of the concept he must once again enunciate. Paul is well aware of the need to warn the Corinthians of the danger of deception. False teachers have been known throughout the history of the church for teaching that God's moral standards are no longer binding or should be reinterpreted.

In his second epistle, Peter speaks of false teachers who "arise among the people" and secretly introduce destructive heresies (2:1). False teachers malign the way of truth (2:2), exploiting others through false words (2:3). Peter describes these false teachers as doing far more than merely mangling words; they are fueled by the sensual rather than the scriptural: "but these like unreasoning animals . . . having eyes full of adultery and that never cease from sin . . . forsaking the right way they have . . . followed the way of Balaam . . . for speaking out arrogant words of vanity they entice by fleshly desires, by sensuality . . . promising freedom while they themselves are slaves of corruption" (2:12, 14–15, 18–19). Jude likewise warned against this very danger (Jude 4).

Paul repeats a basic, almost simplistic axiom: the unrighteous will not inherit the kingdom of God. The kingdom of God is a kingdom of righteousness, just as God is a righteous King. Those who remain in opposition to God and His will cannot expect to be a part of His kingdom. The entire message of the apostle is that God has provided perfect and complete righteousness in the person of Jesus Christ, and that through His saving work on the cross. The cross shows the seriousness of holiness and righteousness to God, and hence to those who would follow Him.

What Paul means by "unrighteous" is explained by the list of vices that makes up the bulk of verses 9 and 10. It is vital to note that the only sin listed in these verses that is *not* likewise listed and identified as a sin in the sight of God in Leviticus 18–20 is drunkenness. Obviously, then, the entire teaching of that passage must be allowed to have its full weight in the interpretation of Paul's list of sins that defines the lives of those who are "unrighteous."

Outside of the constant assertion that the Christian Scriptures are simply not able to address the "modern" concept of homosexuality (including orientation), the controversy over the passage is summed up in the meaning of the term translated by the NASB as homosexuals. The Greek term is *arsenokoites*, and almost every revisionist attempt to remove 1 Corinthians 6:9 (and 1 Timothy 1:10) from the discussion of homosexuality in the Bible is focused on *narrowing* the meaning of this term in such a way as to allow for at least *forms* of homosexual expression if not the entirety of a homosexual lifestyle—a clear case of assuming that which they are trying to prove. As one works through the offerings of Boswell, Scroggs, Countryman, Scanzoni and Mollenkott, and other revisionists, the constant emphasis is on forcing the term into a narrow range that will not have any impact upon "modern" concepts of homosexuality. But can this be done in fairness to the text itself?

The Meaning of Arsenokoites

Why should we believe that the apostle Paul, when he used the term *arsenokoites,* had in mind *any* kind of same-sex activity or practice? Is it not possible that he had in mind something very specific and did not refer to adult, mutual homosexual orientation? Is there any basis for insisting that the term *does* extend to homosexual activity and orientation?

A fair consideration of the writings and background of the apostle Paul reveals that he was well versed in the Greek translation of the Old Testament, the Septuagint (LXX). It was his "Bible," the text he used to share the truth of the gospel as he traveled about the world. While it seems sure that Paul could read the Hebrew as well, he was the apostle to the Gentiles, and the Septuagint was the source of his proclamation and the ground of his defense of the gospel as well. Indeed, at times, when the LXX differed in its wording from the Hebrew text, Paul would choose the LXX, knowing that his audience would have a familiarity with that version. It is a fundamental axiom in all scholarly study of Paul that the LXX is central in the determination of his sources and vocabulary. Truly, no serious challenge can be raised to this simple fact.

The relevance of this truth, however, is seen when we consider the terms that are used in the LXX at Leviticus 18:22 and 20:13. Leviticus 18:22, when transliterated from the LXX Greek into English, in stating that a man shall not lie with a man as one lies with a woman, reads,

> *meta arsenos* (*arsenos*—male) *ou koimethese koiten* (*koiten*—to lie with sexually, have intercourse) *gunaikos.*

But even more striking is the wording of Leviticus 20:13 in the LXX:

> *hos an koimethe meta arsenos koiten gunaikos.*

Note the close connection of *arsenos* (male) and *koiten* (to lie with sexually, have intercourse). The term "homosexual"in 1 Corinthians 6:9 is made up of these two terms, *arsenos* and *koiten*—hence, *arsenokoites*. As a compound word it is clearly referring to male intercourse.

The next fact to consider is also very important. *Arsenokoites* is a term that most agree did not appear prior to its appearance in the New Testament, and specifically in the writings of Paul.[1] So where did it come from? Two possibilities suggest themselves, and both end up having the same impact upon our reading of the text. The term could have derived from rabbinic discussions of homosexuality, based upon the terms *arsenos* and *koiten* in Leviticus 18 and 20. Or it could have been coined by Paul. This would not be unusual at all, for Paul seems to have coined a number of terms based upon the need to communicate the truths of the Hebrew Old Testament in the language of the Greek Septuagint.

James B. DeYoung notes that 179 words found in Paul's writings do not appear in any known pre-Christian literature.[2] Eighty-nine of these appear only once in Paul's writings. Of course, this does not mean that Paul constructed all these terms, but it surely shows a willingness on his part to use what might be called nonstandard terminology to communicate his message. And most importantly, since he draws so heavily and constantly from the LXX itself, the conjunction of the terms *arsenos* and *koiten* (from which *arsenokoites* is derived) proves that the LXX text of Leviticus is the most likely source of this term.

This consideration is further confirmed when we remember that the audience of both letters in which the term *arsenokoites* appears (the Corinthian church and Timothy, Paul's close traveling companion and child in the faith) had direct contact with the apostle's teaching. Paul had spent eighteen months in Corinth, teaching and preaching (Acts 18:1–11). Surely, during this period of time, Paul had spoken to the believers concerning sexual purity as well as sexual immorality.

As we have seen, Corinth was known across the Roman empire as a center of cultic worship that involved sexual debauchery. Temple prostitutes walked the streets, and its citizens knew every form of sexual immorality. Given that Paul would have derived his explanation of God's will for man's sexual behavior from the Scriptures, and specifically from the LXX, the prohibition on homosexuality found in Leviticus 18 and 20 could hardly have been ignored. As was noted above, immediately prior to the discussion in 1 Corinthians 6:9–10, Paul quoted from Deuteronomy 17:7 regarding the removal of the evil man from their midst. His words tell us that the Corinthian believers knew this passage was normative for them, and that they already knew they should have followed its direction. The relevance of this passage in Deuteronomy was a "given," and so, too, the revelation of Leviticus 18 and 20.

Likewise, Timothy, having heard his mentor preaching and teaching on many occasions, having learned the relevance of God's revelation at Paul's feet, would share the same understanding and same common source of reference, the LXX (2 Timothy 3:14–17). As we will see, Paul places his usage of the term *arsenokoites* in his writing to Timothy squarely in the context of the law, which surely would have included Leviticus 18–20.

Having established, then, the context of the word in Paul's usage and its origins in the LXX, we can see why the broad term "homosexual" is the best term to use in translation. The prohibition on homosexual behavior in Leviticus is not restricted to prostitution, or pederasty, or any other subcategory of homosexual immorality. It includes, and condemns, *all* such activity. Since this is the source from which Paul's usage and understanding flows, it follows inevitably that we err when we attempt to limit the scope artificially to any more narrow meaning.[3]

That we have properly identified the term's meaning can be seen by examining the major English renderings of the term. A review of major Bible translations at 1 Corinthians 6:9 reveals that "homosexual" is the translation of the *New American Standard Bible*, the *New Living Translation*, and the *English Standard Version* (in the form of "men who practice homosexuality"). The older but synonymous term "sodomite," is used by the *New King James Version*,[4] the *New Revised Standard Version*, and the *New Jerusalem Bible*. The NIV has "homosexual offenders," and the King James "abusers of themselves with mankind." Likewise, at 1 Timothy 1:10, "homosexual" is the translation of *arsenokoites* in the NASB, NJB, NLT, and ESV (in the form of "men who practice homosexuality"). The term "sodomite" is used by the NKJV and NRSV. The NIV has the less-than-helpful translation "perverts," and the King James has "them that defile themselves with mankind."

We note as well that if homosexuality is an acceptable form of sexual expression (as it is claimed by those who are striving to redefine the Bible's teaching on the subject), *then no other sexual sins beyond adultery and fornication would need to be mentioned.* Yet Paul specifically mentions those who are effeminate and homosexuals as being unrighteous and worthy of God's judgment.

HOPE FOR THE HOMOSEXUAL

We miss the truly redemptive force of 1 Corinthians 6:9–10, however, if we allow ourselves to be caught up solely in the discussion of the meaning of *arsenokoites*. Once its definition has been established, we must surely hear the clear teaching of this portion of God's Word:

> [11]Such were some of you; but you were washed, but you were sanctified, but you were justified in the name of the LORD Jesus Christ, and in the Spirit of our God.

The past tense "such *were* some of you" cannot be ignored. Paul does not address "homosexual Christians." He addresses former homosexuals who were *now* Christians. A transition had taken place, a supernatural movement *from* the practice of homosexuality *to* the Christian faith. They had been *washed*, showing that their previous activities were sinful and required cleansing. They had been sanctified, showing that their previous acts had been unholy. They had been justified, showing that their previous deeds placed them under the wrath of God and made them guilty before Him. But now, by faith in Christ, they had been changed so that they could now look *back* upon a lifestyle that was *no longer theirs*. We must also firmly assert that those who seek to create the untenable label of "homosexual Christian" are in reality *robbing* people of the hope that this passage announces. God cleanses, justifies, and sanctifies those who turn in faith to Jesus Christ. But those who do not turn in faith to Jesus Christ do not experience this divine work.

THE LAW AND TIMOTHY

The apostle Paul cared deeply about the future of the Christian church and showed special concern for the second generation of Christian leaders. His concern is shown in his two letters to Timothy and his single epistle to Titus. Paul knew that the next generation would be facing tremendous challenges, and he obviously desired to make the apostolic message as clear as possible so that it would continue to guide and direct the church.

Paul's work was often opposed by Jews who sought to silence his witness and refute his teaching. He wrote concerning these men in many of his epistles, describing them as those who have wandered away into "vain discussion" (RSV), who while ignorant of the most basic truths of God's law, excel in the demonstration of their ignorance and in the giving of "confident assertions." But upon noting their *misuse* of God's law, Paul reminds Timothy that there is a *proper* use of the law as well. Note his words:

> [8]But we know that the Law is good, if one uses it lawfully, [9]realizing the fact that law is not made for a righteous person, but for those who are lawless and rebellious, for the ungodly and sinners, for the unholy and profane, for those who kill their fathers or mothers, for murderers [10]and immoral men and homosexuals and kidnappers and liars and perjurers, and whatever else is contrary to sound teaching, [11]according to the glorious gospel of the blessed God, with which I have been entrusted.

Paul knows the rightful role of the law in revealing God's holy will and bringing conviction of sin to men (so that they can then be directed to the Savior of sinners, Jesus Christ). The "vice list" that he provides is, of course, not comprehensive. He speaks of "whatever else is contrary to sound teaching" so as to wrap up the entirety of that which is in opposition to God's law, or as he expresses it here, "sound teaching," that he then says is in accordance with "the glorious gospel of the blessed God."

The vice list begins with three pairs of terms that act, in a sense, as a "header" to the list of sins to which Paul refers. They express a wide range of attitudes, all focused on rejection of God's law and standards. "Lawless and rebellious" is the first pair, speaking to those who throw off the constraint of morality and express hatred toward the authority of God. "Ungodly and sinners" refers to those who revel in their rebellion so that they love that which is opposed to godliness and righteousness. "Unholy and profane" continues this line of thought by joining together the preceding pairs: rebels who know God's requirements but fight against them to the point of perverting His truth and profaning His ways may well know what *holiness* means, but they prefer to wallow in the darkness of their sinful and wanton rejection of the path of life.

After these descriptive terms, Paul becomes more specific, listing individual sins. The list is wide ranging, including the murder of one's father or mother, murder in general, immorality in general, kidnapping, lying, and perjuring. In the midst of this description we find *arsenokoites*, "homosexuals." This follows on the heels of "immoral men" (the term used here generally refers to sexually immoral).

It is fitting that homosexual behavior would be included in a list that is headed by the rejection of God's standards for human living. As we have already seen, Paul refers to this kind of behavior as a rebellious "twisting" of God's created order in Romans 1:26–27. The apostle does not need to expand on his descriptive terms: he assumes that Timothy, his child in the faith, a ministering elder in the church, is well aware of the details of the sinful behaviors to which he refers. Timothy would know Paul's teaching on all these subjects, so the mere reference to them is sufficient.

But we should note that Paul refers to homosexuals as those for whom the law was intended, that is, as those who are referred to, rebuked, and shown their sin by the law. And where would the law do this? Clearly in Leviticus 18 and 20. What other context can explain Paul's reference to the right use of the law? This further confirms the meaning of the term and the impropriety of limiting its meaning to a subcategory of same-sex actions, for the source of the term in Leviticus does not allow for this limitation.

The list ends with the comment "and whatever else is contrary to sound teaching." Sound, healthy, proper Christian teaching will speak the truth regarding these kinds of behavior, and if any teaching does *not* do so, it is not truly Christian teaching in the first place. The apostle Paul communicated clearly to the early Christian leaders:

homosexuality is a violation of God's Word, and the Spirit of God recorded this instruction for the benefit of all generations that would follow.

Objection Stated

Arsenokoites *should be defined in a narrow fashion to refer to "male prostitutes."*

Biblical Response

We have already noted this primary objection of revisionist authors[5] or merely to pederasty.[6] But these sources ignore the role of the LXX in the formation of Paul's vocabulary and cannot be taken seriously outside of this consideration. What is more, many revisionists, upon asserting the term is basically beyond our meaningful definition, are forced to fall back on the assertion that the modern view of homosexuality, involving "orientation" and "loving monogamous relationships," was unknown to Paul, and hence what he meant in using *arsenokoites* is for all intents and purposes irrelevant to the modern situation. Revisionist arguments all lead to this singular conclusion: that the biblical text cannot speak to the modern expression of homosexuality. How they support that conclusion may differ, but the goal is always the same.

Even if it could be established that the apostle Paul did not have homosexuality—in act and orientation—in view through his use of the word *arsenokoites*, the clear teaching of the rest of the Bible remains, showing that homosexuality is unacceptable and receives God's judgment.

Objection Stated

Paul is concerned with abuses of excess and is not condemning the proper use of the stated behavior.

For example, the revisionists claim, Paul mentions fornication; this does not mean that sexual relations between members of the opposite sex is wrong—it is the abuse of sexual relations that Paul has in mind. Similarly, Paul mentions idolatry; this does not mean that religious expression or devotion is necessarily wrong. Additionally, Paul mentions adultery; this does not mean that sexual relations within marriage is wrong, it is only the abuse of that relationship that is being condemned as unrighteous. Simply stated, Paul is only dealing with the abuses of homosexual expression and not the proper use or expression of homosexuality.[7]

Biblical Response

Initially we must note that this objection assumes that which it is attempting to prove. This revisionist approach assumes *some* form of acceptable homosexual expression and that this passage is *only* dealing with an abuse of that which is acceptable. A reminder is in order: the Bible *nowhere* approves of homosexual deeds or desires. Nor is there a single example of God's approval of homosexuality.

Additionally, we must observe that this revision of the text, while blind to its invalid circularity, also misses the fact that the apostle Paul is listing the *sinful*, and homosexuality is included in the list. We must, however, more fully consider this idea of excesses and abuse. If Paul is merely listing excesses of that which is acceptable, we should be able to see this with the other deeds listed in the text of 1 Corinthians.

Is there a certain level of *fornication*—devoid of "excess"—that meets with God's approval? How about idolatry . . . does the God who will not give His glory to another tolerate some amount of idolatry? What about the person who asserts that a certain expression of adultery is acceptable just as long as it not *abusive?* Or how about the person who claims that he has an *orientation* toward adultery; should this be approved? Is there an acceptable level of theft? Some appropriate drunkenness? Is it okay to extort on the second Tuesday of every month? Perhaps an *orientation* toward reviling is divinely mandated? Such a drawn out explanation exposes this revision, based upon abuse, to be absurd.

The apostle Paul, consistent with the entirety of the rest of Scripture, clearly shows the sinfulness of homosexuality. The only opacity that surfaces with regard to the terms employed by the apostle is due solely to bias and sexual preference. Paul is not *homophobic* because he categorizes homosexuality as sinful—this must be honestly considered. Paul is no more homophobic than he is *idolophobic, wino-phobic, or adultero-phobic.* Let us imitate the apostle Paul, as he is an imitator of Jesus Christ (1 Corinthians 11:1). Paul properly responded to that which was condemned by the Lord as well as pointed to the only remedy for sinners—Jesus Christ. First Corinthians, chapter six, is clear, and Paul is thinking God's thoughts: homosexuality is sinful and there is hope for the homosexual . . . "for such *were* some of you."

Notes

1. A scan of the relevant material found in the *Thesaurus Linguae Graece CD-Rom* reveals a single use of the term prior to Paul, the infinitival use in the *Sybilline Oracles* (2.73). This work is dated by the TLG canon data as early as the second century B.C. However, the more common dating is A.D. first century. If the material is contemporaneous with Paul, the origin of the term could have come from rabbinic sources, from which Paul could have derived the word as well. And if the material is post-Pauline, its use could have come from Paul or from a common Jewish source.

2. James B. DeYoung, *Homosexuality: Contemporary Claims Examined in the Light of the Bible and Other Ancient Literature and Law* (Grand Rapids: Kregel, 2000), 195.

3. Some scholarly sources limit the meaning in just this way. The impact of political pressures appears even in the realm of Christian scholarship and publishing. For example, the second edition of *A Greek-English Lexicon of the New Testament and Other Early Christian Literature* by Bauer, Arndt, Gingrich, and Danker (University of Chicago, 1979) defines *arsenokoites* as "a male who practices homosexuality, pederast, sodomite" (109). The listed sources were fairly small at this point but included Bailey's work. With the advent of the third edition (now known as *BDAG*) in 2000, the entry more than tripled in size, with the main definition dropping the term "homosexual." The definition given is, "a male who engages in sexual activity w. a pers. of his own sex, *pederast*." The first part of the definition, however, defines a homosexual, not a pederast. The largest portion of added "sources" are revisionist in nature and have already

been addressed. However, *BDAG* does note the formation of the word based upon the LXX usage at Leviticus 20:13, even though this very fact militates strongly against the dropping of the term "homosexual" from the definition (while retaining the description of homosexuality!).

4. The NKJV actually renders another term in this passage, *malakos*, as "homosexual." Many see a connection between *malakos* and *arsenokoites* here, arguing that these terms refer to the passive and active partners in homosexual sexual activity. Even if this is so, the fact that Paul uses *arsenokoites* alone, without *malakos*, at 1 Timothy 1:10, demonstrates the wide meaning of the term, and its proper translation as "homosexual." Compare the *Dictionary of New Testament Theology*: "Paul uses the noun *arsenkoites*, a male homosexual, pederast, sodomite . . . as one who is excluded from the kingdom (1 Cor 6:9) and condemned by the law (1 Tim 1:10; cf. Gen 19; Lev 18:22, 29; 20:13; Deut 23:17)." Colin Brown, ed., *The New International Dictionary of New Testament Theology* (Grand Rapids: Zondervan, 1976), 2:570.

5. This is the assertion of John Boswell, *Christianity, Social Tolerance, and Homosexuality*, 106*ff.* He bases this on a unique reading of the term that must be rejected on many grounds, the primary being that it ignores the LXX background of Paul's use. Likewise, Boswell buttresses his conclusion with even more errant argumentation from the writings of the early Christians. He ignores so many references to major writers that his conclusions are truly without merit. See the discussion by DeYoung, *Homosexuality: Contemporary Claims*, 38. See appendixes B and D of this work, as well as chapter 8. A source that contains much criticism of Boswell's methodologies and research is Robert Gagnon, *The Bible and Homosexual Practice* (Nashville: Abingdon, 2001). See, for example, 344.

6. For example, see Scroggs, *The New Testament and Homosexuality*

(Minneapolis: Fortress Press, 1983), 101–09, 118–22.

7. Daniel Helminiak conceded if 1 Corinthians and 1 Timothy do refer to homosexuality, then "these texts condemn wanton, lewd, irresponsible male homogenital acts but not homogenital acts in general" (*What the Bible Really Says About Homosexuality*, 105). This revisionist approach can also be found in the works of Ralph Blair, *An Evangelical Look at Homosexuality*, and Joseph C. Weber, "Does the Bible Condemn Homosexual Acts?" These works are referred to and critiqued in David E. Malick's article "The Condemnation of Homosexuality in 1 Corinthians 6:9," *Bibliotheca Sacra* 150 (October-December, 1993): 479–92. It is also referred to in John J. McNeill's book *The Church and the Homosexual* (Boston: Beacon Press, 1993), 52.

CHAPTER EIGHT

All You Need Is Love
and Other Justifications

Various other attempts are designed to justify homosexuality as acceptable with biblical morality. When it is shown that the passages that supposedly condemn homosexuality actually *do* condemn homosexuality, then the revisionists must find other ways to defend their preferences. The arguments that follow are those that did not fall precisely into our discussion of the various biblical texts that were surveyed. These arguments, as with the others we have considered, are also put forth as "biblical." These are supposedly based upon the truths of Scripture when taken as a whole. To these we now turn.

Objection Stated

The words "homosexual" and "homosexuality" are not found in the Bible.

This is one of the most common objections raised by those who teach the compatibility of homosexuality and the Bible. This statement has become mantra-like due to its frequency of utterance and is one of the first comments heard from those who argue for the Bible's acceptance of homosexuality. It is presumed that if the Bible *nowhere uses the word homosexuality, it is rather unlikely that the Bible condemns the practice.* We have already seen that this claim is false (see chapter 7) and that the Bible repeatedly condemns homosexual orientation and acts. The Bible unquestionably refers to homosexuality and (this may sound silly) does so by referring to homosexuality. Consider these words from Scanzoni and Mollenkott:

> The Bible does not have a great deal to say about homosexuality, and in the original languages the term itself is never used.[1]

Biblical Response

Frequency of occurrence or repetition does not make something increase in moral reprehensibility. If something is mentioned only one time in all of Scripture and it is labeled abhorrent in that single place, it would remain abhorrent. After all, as far as specific references are concerned, homosexuality is mentioned more often in the Bible than the blasphemy against the Holy Spirit. The blasphemy against the Holy Spirit is known as the "unpardonable sin" and an "eternal sin" (Matthew 12:31; Mark

3:29). Homosexuality is referred to as sin in both the Old and the New Testaments.

Scanzoni and Mollenkott wrote that the term homosexuality is "never used" and "the Bible does not have a great deal to say" about homosexuality. Yet, these authors do admit that the Bible speaks of "homosexual acts."[2] This is striking in its incongruity. Does the Bible have a little to say even if it does not have a "great deal" to say? If the Bible does speak of homosexuality, even a little bit, then the Bible speaks of homosexuality. Perhaps the authors of this apparent contradiction mean to speak of the distinction between act and orientation, between deed and desire. We do recognize a distinction—a functional distinction—between an act and an interest, but we do not recognize an *ethical* or *moral* distinction between a deed and the desire to perform such a deed. The *act* of adultery is immoral as well as the *desire* (lust, longing) to commit adultery (Leviticus 18:20; 20:10; Matthew 5:28; Genesis 39:7–10).[3] The Bible does refer to homosexuality and presents it as something that is morally reprehensible.

Although we strenuously disagree, we are sure that Scanzoni and Mollenkott meant that *an equivalent word* for homosexuality is not found in the original languages when they write, "and in the original languages the term itself is never used." Since the Bible was written in Hebrew[4] and Greek it goes without saying that the *English* word *homosexuality* would not appear in the original languages.

Such a statement fails to recognize that the word used

by the apostle Paul in 1 Corinthians 6:9 and 1 Timothy 1:10 is a compound word that refers to males in bed.[5] We understand that those who are attempting to revise the clear teaching of the Bible claim this word has been improperly translated (see chapter seven), but they are incorrect. We have observed that Paul does use a word that is a legitimately translated by our present English words "homosexual" or "homosexuality." However, there is more. The Bible more often *describes* the behavior that has come to be known as homosexuality. So, although a specific word may not be employed in the majority of the biblical passages, the description of homosexuality most certainly is. As a matter of fact, many early English Bible translations were content to use the word "sodomite" or "buggerer" (one who practices buggery) to refer to homosexuals.[6]

Early English translations of the Bible also employed descriptive phraseology to refer to homosexuals. The *Bishops Bible* of 1575, the *Collins Bible* of 1791, and the *Webster Bible* of 1833 refer to homosexuals as "abusers of themselves with mankind" in 1 Corinthians and as those who "defile themselves with mankind" in 1 Timothy. It is granted, the precise word "homosexual" is not of ancient origin, however, there are plenty of other terms and descriptions that were employed.

Descriptions of homosexuality, rather than the employment of a single word, are found throughout the Bible. In Genesis 19 we find the men of Sodom desiring to have sexual relations with the male visitors in Lot's house. The desire of these townsmen of Sodom is often translated by the words "to know," and, as we saw in chapter 2, this descriptively translates the Hebrew word that refers to an intimate, sexual type of "knowing." Furthermore, the book of Leviticus *describes* the sin of homosexuality as a male lying with a male as one would with a female. The Hebrew word for "lying" is the same word that is used for "bed" or for sexual intercourse elsewhere in the Hebrew Old Testament.[7] Finally, Paul also describes the deeds of homosexuality, thus showing his variety of expression. While he did use a single term in 1 Corinthians and 1 Timothy for homosexuality, he employs descriptive terminology in Romans, chapter 1: "For their women exchanged the natural function for that which is unnatural, and in the same way also the men abandoned the natural function of the woman and burned in their desire toward one another, men with men committing indecent acts and receiving in their own persons the due penalty of their error" (vv. 26–27).

Therefore it is not correct to assert that the Bible does not refer to homosexuality—it most clearly does. However, a final comment in this regard needs to be made. It must be noted that the Bible *nowhere* uses the word "trinity." If, because of this, someone was to assert that the trinity is not biblical because the word "trinity" is not found in the pages of the Bible, we would immediately recognize the unbiblical thinking that was taking place and see an evident departure from the Christian faith.

Objection Stated

Using the Bible to oppose homosexuality is a rather recent occurrence.

Similar to the previous argument about the word "homosexual," it is commonly claimed that the Bible only recently is being interpreted to condemn homosexuality. It is argued that translations of certain passages are being accomplished in accordance with "anti-gay bias" and that such opposition from the church has not always been present. Daniel Helminiak wrote,

> Taken on its own terms and in its own time, the Bible nowhere condemns homosexuality as we know it today. . . . It should be considered outrageous for any educated person to quote the Bible to condemn homosexuality. . . . A millennium ago, Western society was rather indifferent to homosexuality and even supportive of it."[8]

Later he offered these surprising comments:

> Since about the 12th Century, this story [regarding the destruction of Sodom] has been commonly taken to condemn homosexuality. The very word "sodomite" was taken to refer to someone who engages in anal sex, and the sin of Sodom was taken to be male homogenital acts. So supposedly God condemned and punished the citizens of Sodom, the Sodomites, for homogenital activity.[9]

Biblical Response

While it is important to note that truth is not deter-mined by the counting of heads, we will also demonstrate Helminiak's view of history to be inaccurate. Historically, Christian interpretation of the Bible has recognized homosexuality as contrary to God's law and that God's judgment did come upon Sodom, in part, due to homo-sexuality. When Helminiak writes, "since about the 12th Century," he misleads his readers into thinking that *prior to this time* the sins of Sodom were *not* understood to be of a homosexual nature.[10] While it requires *only one* citation that is prior to the twelfth century to refute such a claim, let us consider a number of them.

Athenagorus (second century)

Athenagorus offered a defense of the moral excellence of the Christians in contrast with their accusers. He refers to the "shocking abomination" of male intercourse:

> But though such is our character (Oh! why should I speak of things unfit to be uttered?), the things said of us are an example of the proverb, "The harlot reproves the chaste." For those who have set up a market for for-nication and established infamous resorts for the young for every kind of vile pleasure—who do not abstain even from males, males with males committing shocking abominations, outraging all the noblest and comeliest bodies in all sorts of ways, so dishonoring the fair

workmanship of God (for beauty on earth is not self-made, but sent hither by the hand and will of God)—these men, I say, revile us for the very things which they are conscious of themselves, and ascribe to their own gods, boasting of them as noble deeds, and worthy of the gods. These adulterers and pederasts defame the eunuchs and the once-married (while they themselves live like fishes; for these gulp down whatever falls in their way, and the stronger chases the weaker: and, in fact, this is to feed upon human flesh, to do violence in contravention of the very laws which you and your ancestors, with due care for all that is fair and right, have enacted), so that not even the governors of the provinces sent by you suffice for the hearing of the complaints against those, to whom it even is not lawful, when they are struck, not to offer themselves for more blows, nor when defamed not to bless: for it is not enough to be just (and justice is to return like for like), but it is incumbent on us to be good and patient of evil.[11]

Tertullian (c. 160–225)

Tertullian referred to the deeds of homosexual intimacy in the terms employed by the apostle Paul; they are "against nature." Tertullian also referred to such deeds as contrary to the law of God:

Demanding then a law of God, you have that common one prevailing all over the world, engraven on the natural tables to which the apostle too is wont to appeal, as when in respect of the woman's veil he says, "Does not even Nature teach you?"—as when to the Romans, affirming that the heathen do by nature those things which the law requires, he suggests both natural law and a law-revealing nature. Yes, and also in the first chapter of the epistle he authenticates nature, when he asserts that males and females changed among themselves the natural use of the creature into that which is unnatural, by way of penal retribution for their error.[12]

Origen (c. 185–254)

Origen speaks of those who know the Lord Jesus Christ and declares "that they often exhibit in their character a high degree of gravity, purity, and integrity." On the other hand, those who do not follow Jesus "have despised these virtues and have wallowed in the filth of sodomy, in lawless lust, 'men with men working that which is unseemly.' "[13] In this we see that Origen referred to homosexual acts as sodomy and, contrary to law, they are lawless.

Cyprian (d. 258)

Cyprian spoke of the value of Christian morality and decried the ethical baseness of those who followed lawless lusts. He clearly spoke of homosexual lusts as reprehensible:

> For, their own proper character being overcome, it sends the entire man under its yoke of lust, alluring at first, that it may do the more mischief by its attraction,—

the foe of continency, exhausting both means and modesty; the perilous madness of lust frequently attaining to the blood, the destruction of a good conscience, the mother of impenitence, the ruin of a more virtuous age, the disgrace of one's race, driving away all confidence in blood and family, intruding one's own children upon the affections of strangers, interpolating the offspring of an unknown and corrupted stock into the testaments of others. And this also, very frequently burning without reference to sex, and not restraining itself within the permitted limits, thinks it little satisfaction to itself, unless even in the bodies of men it seeks, not a new pleasure, but goes in quest of extraordinary and revolting extravagances, contrary to nature itself, of men with men.[14]

These church fathers, all of them prior to the twelfth century, are clear: homosexuality is contrary to the law of God, it is against nature, and it is not consistent with biblical morality. These fathers appealed to an abiding standard of morality (God's law) and declared homosexuality to be contrary to it. They also referred to homosexuality as being part of the sin of Sodom. One could also refer to the writings of Lactantius,[15] Eusebius,[16] Athanasius,[17] Chrysostom,[18] and Augustine[19] and find the same conclusions.[20]

These results are consistent with those preached in Chrysostom's *Fourth Homily on the Epistle to the Romans* and are worth reading today (this homily is reproduced in its entirety in appendix B). The claim that the Bible prohibits homosexuality is *not* a recent development. It is the Christian interpretation of antiquity.[21]

Objection Stated

"All you need is love." *But this is consensual. We're not harming anyone.*

Biblical Response

"All You Need Is Love" is a Beatles song that does not make for good theology or ethics. We will not argue about the prominent place of love in Christian theology and practice; without it we would not have redemption (John 3:16; Romans 5:8; 1 John 4:10). Nor will we argue about the Christian requirement that we love one another. It is unquestionably Christian doctrine that "the one who loves his brother abides in the light" (1 John 2:10). Furthermore, "we know that we have passed out of death into life because we love the brethren" (1 John 3:14). We agree that we should "not love with word or with tongue, but in deed and truth" (1 John 3:18). The loving of one another is evidence of the life of God abiding in us (1 John 4:12). Truly, "we love, because He first loved us" (1 John 4:19), and we must love one another if we truly love God (1 John 4:20).

While these passages are ringing in our ears, we are accused of acting in an unloving or unchristian way when we express our disagreement with persons who are practicing or pursuing homosexuality. This is a special favorite of persons in the church who presume the compatibility of their homosexual lifestyle with biblical morality. These folks claim that "the chief Christian virtue" of love is being violated by those who disagree with their homosexual preference. We are being told, "So long as the parties involved in the 'union' are loving, just so long as they are committed, it's no big deal." After all, "all you need is love." The ultimate question at this point is, what does it mean to be loving?

The authors of this book are in complete agreement with the teaching of Scripture that says we must love one another, even our enemies (Matthew 5:44). We ought not to engage in conduct devoid of Christian charity. But what does this look like? Is it loving to "live and let live?" Is it loving never to share a correction, a reproof, or an admonition? Is it loving to turn away and ignore that which we know to be true? Is it loving to know what the Word of God says about a particular subject and not share it with those for whom you are concerned, due to a fear of conflict? Just what does the Bible mean when it calls upon us to act lovingly?

To love one another, to behave lovingly, is to—stating the matter as simply as possible—do *what* God says to do in the *way* God says to do it. Or, to put it another way, we must do the right thing, in the right way. To be loving is to be *lawful*: to obey God's commands. "For this is the love of God, that we keep His commandments, and His commandments are not burdensome" (1 John 5:3). The love of God first comes to us so that we are enabled to love one another, and the exhibition of our love for God is defined as the keeping of His commandments. Paul wrote, "Love . . . is the fulfillment of the law" (Romans 13:10). One of God's commandments prohibits homosexuality (Leviticus 18:22; 20:13). Love of God, since it follows God's commands, requires the cessation of homosexual practices. The love of God compels others, who are not homosexual, to present faithful instruction and admonition from God's Word to those who are engaged in the sin of homosexuality. This is an exhibition of the love of God.

This is the very thing we have attempted to do in this book. We are not homophobic, nor are we haters of homosexuals. Disagreement with the morality of homosexuality does not make one hateful or homophobic. Showing the clear teaching of God's Word—the admitted authority for those on both sides of this same-sex controversy—is loving: "Better is open rebuke than love that is concealed" (Proverbs 27:5). As Christian ministers we appeal to those who are practicing or pursuing homosexuality: you must obey God and repent. To pursue that which is under God's condemnation is not a kinky satisfaction, nor is it harmless. To live a life contrary to God's Word—a life of homosexuality—is to declare that which is evil to be good, and the good to be evil. It is naïve and unbiblical to assume that sins occur in a vacuum, in isolation from others. "Righteousness exalts a nation, but sin is a disgrace to any people" (Proverbs 14:34). If you claim to be a Christian, if the love of God has first invaded your life, then you *must* obey His commands. You must live in accordance with His standards of morality and forsake the interest and engagement in homosexuality. In the case before us, we should exhibit our disagreement in a loving way . . . and the truth has been declared.

Objection Stated

But this is the way that God made me.

Those who assert the compatibility of their homosexuality with biblical morality claim that their condition is due to nature, not nurture. They want others to believe that their homosexuality is a matter of genetics.

Biblical Response

This book is designed to deal with arguments for homosexuality that are supposedly derived from the Bible, and we have dealt with the passages that are concerned with this topic. While an in-depth consideration of the scientific data on this topic is far beyond the scope of this book, we do have two responses to make. First, the data is inconclusive to prove that a predisposition to homosexuality is genetic—it simply has not been proven. And secondly, even if homosexuality were due to one's nature, caused by the way one is made, this says *nothing about the moral acceptability of the practice.*

Those who assert that homosexuality is simply a matter of genetics must deal with the fact that there is a vast difference between *disposition* and *necessity*. That is, even if we were to grant the argument that genetics in some way is relevant to homosexual desire or behavior, it is a long stretch to move from being *predisposed* to homosexuality and finding homosexual behavior *necessary*. Even societies that reject Christian standards do not accept this kind of thinking: saying a person is "predisposed" to murder is not a valid excuse for anyone to murder someone. Every human being can claim some kind of "disposition" to one sin or another; the fact remains that God holds men accountable for their actions, even when that involves fighting *against* the "lusts of the flesh." The Lord Jesus did not accept as a valid excuse for lusting after a woman: "Men are predisposed to lust. We are made that way." Jesus taught that we are to battle the lusts of the flesh:

> You have heard that it was said, "YOU SHALL NOT COMMIT ADULTERY"; but I say to you that everyone who looks at a woman to lust for her has already committed adultery with her in his heart. And if your right eye makes you stumble, tear it out, and throw it from you; for it is better for you that one of the parts of your body perish, than for your whole body to be thrown into hell. And if your right hand makes you stumble, cut it off, and throw it from you; for it is better for you that one of the parts of your body perish, than for your whole body to go into hell. (Matthew 5:28–30)

Surely the Lord's words speak of a battle against lust and desire, but there is no room given for excuses based upon "predisposition." While we all have those sins to which our constitution makes us more vulnerable (pride, arrogance, lust, and greed, to name a few), this never gives us an excuse, nor does it release us from the wrath of God against that sin. So even if we grant some kind of predisposition, whether genetic or contextual, such a predisposition would *not* excuse the desires or the activity. All of us were born as descendants of Adam and are sinners. Our natural inclination—*predisposition*, if the term is preferred—is to sin; we sin because we are sinners. However, this natural bent to sin does not free us from the responsibility of—or the guilt from—the sins we commit. So, even if we were to grant some type of "nature over nurture" proclivity toward homosexuality, it does nothing to establish the acceptability of the practice and does everything to show responsibility.[22]

But there is truly no reason to grant the genetic argument in the first place.[23] Many in the homosexual movement are realizing that such an apologetic is actually detrimental to their cause, though they at first embraced inconclusive studies as if they were the final word on the matter. God surely created us as we are. As the psalmist said, "For it was you who formed my inward parts; you knit me together in my mother's womb" (Psalm 139:13 NRSV). But to assert that God made us in such a way that we must of *necessity* live in a manner that dishonors Him goes directly against biblical teaching.

Objection Stated

As a loving couple, we should be allowed to marry in the church if we so choose.

Homosexuals commonly demand their "rights," which include the desire to be recognized as legitimate couples, who should be allowed to marry if they wish.

Biblical Response

This recognition of homosexual marriage is something that the church cannot allow and remain faithful to the God of truth. It is not evidence of compassion to allow others to openly violate the clear teaching of the Bible. Yes, it is "tolerant"—that is without question—but what about asking whether or not God would allow tolerance on other ethical matters? "Tolerance" is today's "sacred cow": the values of many fashioned into something false. While the modern view of tolerance may be applauded as "progressive," it is actually damning. Scripture describes those who practice the violation of the marriage covenant as taking steps that lead to Sheol; they live in accordance with death and damnation (see Proverbs 5:3–6; 7:6–27). If this is the case with those who practice the deeds, what about those who encourage such behavior through false teaching? A greater punishment comes upon the teachers of falsehood (Matthew 18:6; James 3:1; 2 Peter 2:21).

The church is "the pillar and support of the truth" (1 Timothy 3:15) and must therefore adhere to and speak the truth concerning God's institution of marriage. To do so is not unloving, judgmental, or hateful; it is loving, discerning, and faithful.

Marriage is God's institution. God invented it. God has

set its terms, and no one has the right to alter them according to his own whim or preference. When we speak of God's institution of marriage, we ought to speak of it in accordance with His own Word. How does God describe marriage? It is the union between a man and a woman. God is the one who has determined the nature of marriage. Seeing this, we will find homosexual marriages precluded.

Covenant, Complement, and Children

What is the truth about marriage? Biblically considered, marriage is to be between one man and one woman. A *man* is to leave his father and mother and cleave to his *wife*. One man and one woman are to become one flesh; they are to be joined together (Genesis 2:24). In marriage, the man and the woman are united in what the Bible calls a covenant (Malachi 2:14; Proverbs 2:17). The covenant is something that they have entered into. It is something outside of the man and woman; it is not of their design. This covenant is God's design, and He has nowhere designed such a covenant for members of the same sex. Furthermore, the man and the woman are to be complementary to one another; they are to work together in the ways that God has prescribed (Genesis 1:27–29; 2:20–24; Proverbs 31:10–31; 1 Corinthians 7:2–5). Part of this "complementariness" is seen in the role of the married man and woman in their ability to produce children, solely possible with two sexes (Genesis 1:28; Malachi 2:15).

Many marriages are found in the Bible. A homosexual "marriage" is not a covenant ordained by God, it is not complementary (being the same), and it lacks the ability to produce children—it is a non-perpetuating entity. This fact can be seen from another angle: children are to have *parents*, and in the Bible these are called "father and mother" (Exodus 20:12; Luke 18:20; Mark 7:10–12; Ephesians 6:1–2). Every instance of marriage in the Bible is heterosexual, because no homosexual union can be considered marriage. Every time divorce—the dissolution of a marriage between persons—is mentioned in the Bible, it is between a man and a woman.

In Ephesians 5, we find the example, the pattern, for all marriages. This pattern is one that is between Christ and the church, which is His bride (Ephesians 5:22–32). The picture of marriage that God places before us is one between a bridegroom and a bride—this is the case throughout the Bible. Marriage is a covenant designed by God and, as such, God has set the terms of this institution that He has designed. According to His designation, marriage is to be between a man and a woman. No alternatives are acceptable.

Additionally, the Lord Jesus referred to marriage as that which occurs between one man and one woman, whether in response to a question or used in instruction (Matthew 22:23–30; Luke 16:18). Most important in this regard is the fact that the Lord Jesus Christ allowed the description of marriage as being between a man and his wife to stand uncontested (Matthew 19:10). Many people in the homosexual community are tired of hearing comments about marriage being exclusively between one man and one woman. This fact is revealing. Much is seen about people's willingness to submit to the authority of the Bible by observing their attitude toward the Bible. As Christians we submit to what the Bible teaches, including its teaching on marriage. While the authors of this book agree that off-hand comments about "Adam and Steve" or "Ava and Eve" ought to be discontinued (they rarely, if ever, contribute to meaningful discussion), we do not think that we should cease dealing with what the Bible has to say about marriage. The question before us is whether or not we will lead our lives in accordance with the clear teaching and instruction of the Bible.

But Don't Scholars Say?

An Example in Evaluation

The oft-repeated mantra "Scholarship has spoken, the case is closed" can bring great pressure to bear upon the Christian who seeks to be faithful to the Word's moral imperatives. And while many are beginning to understand the need to hear what "scholars" say within a more discerning context (witness the rapid rise of the "intelligent design" movement and the inroads it has made within culture as a whole), the issue arises with more force when

"Christian scholarship" speaks with a divided voice.

This is surely the case when the issue of homosexuality and the abiding relevance of God's moral law in our lives is under discussion. Many struggle to understand how scholars can know the Word with such depth, understand its backgrounds and its languages, and still conclude that behaviors such as homosexuality are viable alternatives for the believer.

A compilation of articles by scholars at Princeton Seminary on the subject of homosexuality appeared in 1996, titled *Homosexuality and Christian Community*. The work was edited by Choon-Leong Seow, an Old Testament scholar and author of the widely used beginning Hebrew grammar *A Grammar for Biblical Hebrew*. Seow authored a chapter titled "A Heterosexual Perspective." We have chosen to examine his conclusions as a very helpful example of how it is that scholars who study the Christian Scriptures can come to such widely divergent conclusions on the issue of homosexuality.

The argumentation presented in the bulk of Seow's chapter has already been dealt with in this book. And while it might be useful to examine specific elements of the argumentation where Seow presents an unusual twist or turn, the real reasons for the argumentation presented flow clearly from the final portion of the chapter—"Some Personal Observations." Unlike so much of the literature that is available today, this section provides a vital and important personal insight into the factors that determine how a scholar determines what kind of weight to assign to

Scripture, personal experience, and cultural issues. We quote from Seow:

> The sages recognize that neither human observation nor experiences can be absolutely reliable. There are some risks when one turns to them. Yet it is necessary for people to live with risks; we have no choice in the matter, for there are still many things in creation that are not revealed to us.[24]

That is quite true, but the nature of our own beings, our sexual expressions, and our moral behavior are not included in the "mysteries" that are not revealed. Appealing to "mystery" when the Word is clear and sufficient in its statements is unnecessary, and always dangerous.

> God is in Wholly Other, but we are mere mortals. We cannot be too sure that we know the ways of God.[25]

At this point we truly have to ask what role God's work of inspiration by His Spirit plays in the giving of Scripture. Surely God's ways are past finding out *unless* He chooses to reveal them, and when we speak of His will concerning the behavior of His creatures, surely we must believe God is capable of making His will known with clarity.

> We take the risks because we are human. Like the sages who gave us the wisdom tradition, we live knowing that what we see and experience often contradicts what we have always thought to be true. Since the wisdom tradition points us beyond texts to consider observation and experience, I want to conclude by telling of my own experience.[26]

While wisdom literature may speak of observation and experience, it does not tell us God is not capable of revealing His will, nor does it tell us that God's truth is mutable and changing. As we will see in the words that follow, the central issue will become "Which authority is final: my interpretation of my personal experience, or the revelation of God in Scripture?"

> I used to believe that divorce is wrong under any circumstance, simply because that is what the scriptures teach. I could—and still can—quote chapter and verse from the Bible, particularly the words of Jesus.[27]

Since Jesus allowed for exceptions based upon *porneia*, "fornication" (Matthew 5:32), and the apostle Paul recognized that unbelievers might leave believing spouses, it is hard to understand exactly why Dr. Seow says "any circumstance."

> I have since learned from friends and loved ones what horrible traps bad marriages can be. People suffer enormously; some people even kill themselves because of bad marriages that they cannot otherwise escape. Some people suffer physical abuse in such marriages. Some are even killed.[28]

A bad marriage can be a horrible situation. Suicide is a terrible thing. But it is surely without merit to connect an errant understanding of scriptural teaching (as noted above) with *forcing* people into situations of abuse or violence.

> Unlike the friends of Job, I am not willing to uphold
> dogma at all costs, certainly not when I know that people
> are suffering and dying. I have gone back to reread the
> scriptures and I have heard the gospel anew.[29]

What does it mean to "hear the gospel anew"? Does it mean "I realized that I had misunderstood passages such as Matthew 5:32 and 1 Corinthians 7:15, and that, in fact, God's Word was not to blame for these things"? Or does it mean "I have chosen to override biblical imperatives in light of my own interpretation of experience and Scripture itself"? If the gospel is the message of God's wondrous work in Jesus Christ, does it change to "fit" each passing generation's "felt needs"? Or is it a timeless and unchanging message, one that calls us to obedience?

> I also used to believe that homosexual acts are always
> wrong.[30]

The parallel drawn here is clear: once Dr. Seow believed every instance of divorce to be wrong, but he has "heard the gospel anew" and has moved beyond "dogma." And he once believed that homosexual acts were always wrong, just like all divorces were wrong. Of course, one could immediately point out that divorce and homosexuality are not parallel issues: homosexuality involves sexual activity, choices, and proclivities, while divorce can have any number of divergent factors that far transcend the choices involved in homosexuality.

Listening to gay and lesbian students and friends, however, I have had to rethink my position and reread the scriptures.[31]

Do we read the Scriptures so as to hear what *they* say, or to hear what others are saying? Should not what we hear from the Spirit in His Word inform how we hear what others say, or should what others say cause us to "reread" the Scriptures? Which is the ultimate authority?

Seeing how gay and lesbian people suffer discrimination, face the rejection of family and friends, risk losing their jobs, and live in fear of being humiliated and bashed, I cannot see how anyone would prefer to live that way. I do not understand it all, but I am persuaded that it is not a matter of choice.[32]

Sin harms human beings. It distorts and twists and destroys. And despite the consistent testimony of all humankind from the beginning, man keeps sinning, despite all the agony, alienation, fear, and pain sin causes. To conclude that homosexuality must be a part of God's creative purpose, so that there are "gay and lesbian Christians" (the conclusion of this line of reasoning) is illogical. Pedophiles receive even worse treatment, yet they still practice their sin. Are we to assume they do not choose to do so? What of Paul's direct statement that this *is* a chosen act, one reflective of the suppression of the knowledge of God and idolatry? We see here a clear opportunity for making a choice between whether we will allow the Word to determine our worldview and our conclusions, or whether we will subjugate the Word to our own feelings, our own thoughts. The ramifications of our decision are far reaching indeed.

> Seeing how some gay and lesbian couples relate to one another in loving partnerships, observing how much joy they find in one another, and seeing that some of them are better parents than most of us ever will be, I have reconsidered my views. I was wrong.[33]

For the one whose worldview is forged upon the revelation of God in Scripture, these words seem very foreign and almost unintelligible. What is a gay "couple," given God's design of man and woman? How can one describe such a relationship as a "loving partnership" when the correspondence God himself created in the man/woman relationship is not only absent but also denied? How is it loving to attempt to relate to a mirror image? Does this not violate the very categories of love defined by Scripture itself? What does it mean to say that one can find joy in the suppression of God's truth and the twisting of His creative decree? Is this the kind of abiding joy of which the Word speaks, or is it a substitute? How can two men or two women act as "parents" when the very term from the dawn of creation has referred, in its plural form, to a father and a mother? How can true loving and sacrifice and giving be modeled before children in such a relationship? And what does it mean to reconsider one's views on the basis of emotional responses to such unusual and unnatural relationships rather than upon the basis of God's revelation?

> From the testimony of homosexual persons and from
> various reports, I have learned that there is an extraor-
> dinarily high rate of suicide among homosexual persons.
> People are dying every day because of society's atti-
> tudes—indeed, because of the church's stance.[34]

Upon what basis does Dr. Seow conclude that his observation of a higher than normal suicide rate provides sufficient basis for an accusation against society in general and the church in particular? Did the possibility that the lifestyle itself—which requires a tremendous output of energy for the maintenance of the suppression of God's truth and the voice of conscience—ever come to mind as the actual trigger mechanism? Is it possible that Dr. Seow has misinterpreted what he has seen, and that the "joy" to which he referred is in reality empty and shallow? The creature made in God's image cannot truly enjoy the twist-ing of that image on a daily basis.

Further, are we to believe that the church's stance is to be determined by continuous, emotionally based observa-tion of changing social norms rather than upon an unchanging base of revelation? This seems the only possi-ble conclusion from this kind of approach.

> Many people hate themselves because of what society
> and the church say about them.[35]

Is it possible that this self-loathing is generated by the lifestyle itself, which forces a person to live contrary to God's creative design, so that when such a person is reminded of their rebellion and their internal pain and misery by outside elements, whether by the church or society, they make an unwarranted connection?

> I know of many homosexual persons in the ministry who have been very effective for the cause of Jesus Christ, but they suffer tremendous guilt because they have kept their secret from the church they love dearly.[36]

How does one even *define* the "cause of Jesus Christ" outside of scriptural norms, the very norms being abandoned through the appeal to personal experience by Dr. Seow in these words? How "effective" is one in preaching God's truth in Christ, who has confirmed the validity of the revelation of sin, punishment, and wrath (the very background of the cross of Christ) when one continues in a lifestyle that Paul identified as a *past-tense* experience in the life of some in the fellowship at Corinth (*not* a present-tense, ongoing lifestyle)? And if we love the church, will that love not cause us to seek to honor the Lord and *all* of His teachings?

> I have met many students here at the Princeton Seminary who have a strong sense of the call and all the obvious gifts for it, but they cannot obey their call because of who they are. They are hurt by the church.[37]

This kind of argumentation utterly overthrows any basis for meaningful moral standards in the church of Jesus Christ. It not only places the "call" solely in the human realm, making it a subjective thing that is separated from any objective standards (such as those laid out in Scripture in 1 Timothy and Titus), but it seemingly suggests that if the church is faithful to the Word and its imperatives, the church is placed in a position of standing *against* the work of the Spirit in "calling" such a person to ministry. This inconceivable contradiction is created solely by the insertion of Dr. Seow's personal observations on a level *above* Scripture, so that the very idea of a "homosexual person" in the sense of one who is so in a morally neutral, or even positive, way is allowed to override the clear biblical norms we have already examined.

> I cannot believe that we are called to perpetuate such pain and suffering in the world. I am compelled now to trust my observations and experience.[38]

Does the church of Jesus Christ perpetuate pain and suffering through her fidelity to God's truth, or do men and women perpetuate their own pain and suffering by continuing in their slavery to sin and in their suppression of God's truth?

> For me there is nothing less than the gospel at stake. I have no choice but to take the testimonies of gays and lesbians seriously. I do so with some comfort, however, for the scriptures themselves give me the warrant to trust that human beings can know truths apart from divine revelation.[39]

We can surely agree that nothing less than the gospel is at stake here. But in the next sentence Dr. Seow tells us that he places as his highest authority not the Scriptures that give us the gospel, but the testimony of gays and lesbians. He thinks the Scriptures give him a warrant to do this by saying that we can know truths apart from divine revelation. Of course we can. But we cannot know divine truths in *contradiction* to divine revelation. And that is what we have when Dr. Seow "rereads" the gospel and places his interactions with homosexuals as the lens through which God's objective revelation must pass. The wisdom writers did not seek to encourage us to contradict God's clear revelation. The truths we are to learn are truths of wisdom; the wise man does not place his experience and feelings above God's truth, but instead interprets them in the light of revelation, ordering and prioritizing what he learns with reference to the unchanging standard of God's Word, upon which he meditates day and night.

Notes

1. Scanzoni and Mollenkott, *Is the Homosexual My Neighbor*, 54.
2. Ibid., 60.
3. It is interesting to note with regard to this issue of deed and desire that the townsmen of Sodom were *desirous* of sexual intimacy with the men who were lodging in Lot's home; they did not engage in any deeds of sexual intimacy at all and they were yet accused of "great wickedness."
4. Some of the Old Testament was written in Aramaic as well.
5. Paul uses the word *arsenokoites*, which is a compound word of *arsen*, meaning man or male, and *koite*, which means bed or intercourse and is where we derive our word "coitus." Paul uses a word that refers to male intercourse and it is the very same word used in Leviticus 18:22 and 20:13 in the Septuagint.
6. See the Geneva Bible of 1560 (1 Kings 14:24; 15:12; 22:46; 1 Kings 23:7; 1 Corinthians 6:9; and 1 Timothy 1:10).
7. The Hebrew word is *mish-cov*. Compare Leviticus 18:22 and 20:13 with Numbers 31:17–18, 35, and Judges 21:11–12.
8. *What the Bible Really Says About Homosexuality*, 13, 23.
9. Ibid., 44.
10. In his book *Christianity, Social Tolerance, and Homosexuality*, John Boswell argued similarly: "Within a few generations of the first disciples, the majority of converts to Christianity were not Jews, and their attitude toward Jewish law was to say the least ambivalent. Most Christians regarded the Old Testament as an elaborate metaphor for Christian revelation; extremely few considered it morally binding in particular details" (102). Later Boswell comments, "Almost no early Christian writers appealed to Leviticus as authority against homosexual acts . . . it would

simply not have occurred to most early Christians to invoke the authority of the old law to justify the morality of the new" (104–05). This is patently false and reveals Boswell's misunderstanding of the relationship between law and grace (see appendix A). The nationality of the converts to Christianity did not change the basis for moral behavior. The writers of the New Testament, even those who ministered primarily to Gentiles, faithfully appealed to the Old Testament law in support of their instruction. It is simply not true to accuse them of "ambivalence" with regard to the "old law." Paul, the apostle to the Gentiles (Galatians 2:7–9), instructed the Gentile churches—by quotation and application—with the law of Moses (see Romans 7:7–12; 13:7–10; 1 Corinthians 7:19; 9:9–14; Galatians 5:14; Ephesians 6:2; 1 Timothy 5:18–19). On the contrary, it is Boswell who views the Old Testament law with ambivalence.

11. *The Ante-Nicene Fathers,* volume 2; Fathers of the Second Century: Athenagorus, chapter 34, 147.

12. *The Ante-Nicene Fathers,* volume 3; Tertullian, *The Chaplet, or De Corona,* chapter 6, 96.

13. *The Ante-Nicene Fathers,* volume 4; Origen, *Against Celsus,* book 7, chapter 49, 631.

14. *The Ante-Nicene Fathers,* volume 5; Cyprian, *The Treatises of Cyprian—"Of the Discipline and Advantage of Chastity,"* 588.

15. *The Ante-Nicene Fathers,* volume 7; Fathers of the Third and Fourth Centuries: Lactantius, *The Divine Institutes,* book 1, chapter 11, 20; and *Of the Manner in Which the Persecutors Died,* volume 7, chapter 8, 303–04.

16. *The Nicene and Post-Nicene Fathers,* second series, volume 1; Church History of Eusebius: *"The Oration of Eusebius Pamphilus, in Praise of the Emperor Constantine,"* chapter 13, 600–03.

17. *The Nicene and Post-Nicene Fathers,* second series, volume 4; Athanasius: *Select Writings and Letters, Against the Heathen,* 26, 17–18. See

also, *Select Writings and Letters, "On the Incarnation of the Word"*, volume 4, section 5, 38–39.

18. *The Nicene and Post-Nicene Fathers*, volume 11; Chrysostom: *Homilies on the Acts of the Apostles and the Epistle to the Romans—Homily 4 on Romans 1:26–27*, 355–59. See also *The Nicene and Post-Nicene Fathers*, volume 12; Chrysostom: *Homilies on the Epistles of Paul to the Corinthians—Homily 26 on 1 Corinthians 11:2 (verse 15)*, 154.

19. *The Nicene and Post-Nicene Fathers*, volume 5; Augustin's Anti-Pelagian Works: *The Merits and Forgiveness of Sins and on the Baptism of Infants—"Sin and the Penalty of Sin the Same,"* book 3, chapter 24 [xxii], 129. See also *The Nicene and Post-Nicene Fathers*, volume 5; Augustin's Anti-Pelagian Works: *On Marriage and Concupiscence—"He Answers the Arguments of Julianus,"* book 2, chapter 35 [xxx]. What is the Natural Use of the Woman? What is the Unnatural Use? 297.

20. Concerning the city of Sodom, see the *Epistle to the Corinthians* by Clement of Rome (*The Apostolic Fathers*, 46) and Irenaeus's *Against Heresies* (*The Ante-Nicene Fathers*, volume 1, 504*ff*, book IV.31.1 and 3). One should also reference Josephus (c. 37–100) in this regard. Although he is not a church father, he is a writer of antiquity and spoke unambiguously regarding the sins of Sodom and the destruction of that city. Consider the following citations from his works:

[While commenting on the location of Lake Asphaltitis, he mentions] "The country of Sodom borders upon it. It was of old a most happy land, both for the fruits it bore and the riches of its cities, although it be now all burnt up. It is related how, for the impiety of its inhabitants, it was burnt by lightning; in consequence of which there are still the remainders of that Divine fire, and the traces [or shadows] of the five cities are still to be seen, as well as the ashes growing in their fruits; which fruits have a colour as if they were fit to be eaten, but if you pluck them with your hands, they dissolve into smoke and ashes. And thus what is related of this land of Sodom hath these marks of credibility which our very sight affords us" (*Wars of the Jews*, Book IV.8.4).

"About this time the Sodomites grew proud, on account of their riches and great wealth; they became unjust towards men, and impious towards God, insomuch that they did not call to mind the advantages they received from him: they hated strangers, and abused themselves with Sodomitical practices. God was therefore much displeased at them, and determined to overthrow their city, and to lay waste their country, until there should neither plant nor fruit grow out of it" (*Antiquities of the Jews*, Book 1, XI.1).

Furthermore, the pillar of salt, which was Lot's wife, was still standing during the lifetime of Josephus: "for I have seen it, and it remains at this day" (*Antiquities*, Book 1, XI.4).

21. Contrary to popular opinion, homosexuality was *not* accepted in nonchristian cultures of antiquity as many would have us believe. In Suetonius's *The Twelve Caesars*, we read of Julius Caesar's apparent homosexuality with King Nicomedes as something that was "always a dark stain on his reputation and frequently quoted by his enemies" (35).

22. A vile and disturbing consistency of this nature is found in the book by Randy Thornhill and Craig Palmer, *A Natural History of Rape* (The MIT Press). While the authors do not contend that rape is morally right, they do argue that Darwinian evolutionary biology can explain human behavior, including the crime of rape. These authors argue that evolved adapation of some sort give rise to rape. This line of thinking is frightful. To claim that one's behavior is "genetic" or part of a person's make-up is the precursor to arguing for its social acceptability and, eventually, civil protection. Although Thornhill and Palmer are

merely following their Darwinian fiction to its logical conclusions, most can still see the moral reprehensibility of rape. Our point is simple: even *if* someone was predisposed to a certain type of immoral behavior, such a predisposition does not make the behavior any less immoral.

23. We note in passing the incongruity of the genetic argument for those homosexuals who embrace a neo-Darwinian evolutionary view of the origins and nature of biological life. A "gay gene" would, in any neo-Darwinian scheme, be automatically selected against, as it would result in the person carrying such a gene to have no offspring, the very opposite "goal" of the evolutionary scheme. As a result, even if such a gene existed, it would be removed from the genetic pool of the species over time by natural selection, and could only reappear as a result of mutation. If one argues that it could be a recessive gene that appears only rarely, such as is seen in some genetic diseases, this is hardly helpful to the cause, as this would result not only in viewing homosexuality as a genetic disease, but it would militate strongly against the claims of the homosexual movement regarding the allegedly high percentage of homosexuals in the population.

24. Choon-Leong Seow, ed., *Homosexuality and Christian Community* (Louisville: Westminster John Knox Press, 1996), 24.

25. Ibid.

26. Ibid.

27. Ibid.

28. Ibid., 25.

29. Ibid.

30. Ibid.

31. Ibid.

32. Ibid.

33. Ibid.

34. Ibid.
35. Ibid.
36. Ibid.
37. Ibid.
38. Ibid.
39. Ibid.

CHAPTER NINE

Conclusion: A Pastoral Appeal

This chapter is written as an appeal, by two ordained ministers, to people who are struggling with homosexual practices or desires. As this book has shown, the biblical data regarding homosexuality clearly indicates that it is sinful and not acceptable to God. Obedience to the Word of God is required of all persons and is the delighted, privileged employment of those who bear the name of the Lord. Though obedience offers great benefit to those who know it, it is not merely an option. Since we are chiefly dealing with the same-sex controversy as it pertains to the church, the only issue before us now is one of obedience: will God's Word be obeyed, or will it be twisted to defend a cherished "sexual preference"?

Though many good reasons exist for you to forsake homosexual practices, we urge you to forsake them for the main reason: they are displeasing to God. Repentance is the only option before you. Despite the arguments that exist to the contrary, homosexuality is not natural, is not approved by the Word of God, and is a practice that leads to death. The Bible clearly teaches that homosexuality, whether in interest or practice, is sin. We deny that recognizing something as sinful when God has declared it sinful is therefore hateful. By recognizing homosexuality to be sinful, however, we do not seek to self-righteously condemn anyone. We do not desire to be excessively harsh. We are simply pointing to the *only* hope for those struggling with homosexuality.

Calling homosexuality a sin will seem to be a cruel, insensitive attitude, a "homophobic response" of condemnation rather than concern. But the truth is that it is the beginning of true freedom and joy for the homosexual. For if homosexuality were either an inescapable human condition (like height and skin color) or an incurable disease, there would be no hope. The homosexual would be locked in his lusts forever, with no possibility of escape. Once we see clearly that homosexuality is a sin, we can also see the way of deliverance.[1]

We wish to be perfectly clear: homosexuality is not the unpardonable sin. Homosexuals can be forgiven. This truth must be kept in mind both by those who are involved in homosexual behavior and those who are not. Perhaps out of revulsion, or out of a cloister mentality, the church has failed to speak the truth or apply God's remedial mercy. Instead, the church must remain faithful to the teaching of God's Word; she cannot condone that which God condemns, and she must illuminate the path of repentance.

That homosexuality is a sin means that it is *only* a sin—nothing more. It is not some mystical force within the person, some genetic or psychological programming that cannot be overcome. It is a transgression of God's law, a form of self-love that expresses itself in a particularly heinous attack on God's image.[2]

Repentance, change, and hope are possible. Release from enslavement to homosexuality is the great desire of all but the most jaded homosexuals. We have seen the evidence in their eyes and in their speech; their conscience bears witness that the law of God is written on their hearts and that they are in violation of it (Romans 2:15). The apostle Paul, while remaining true to what God declares about sin, spoke of some members of the Corinthian church who had been freed from their slavery to the sin of homosexuality.

Or do you not know that the unrighteous shall not inherit the kingdom of God? Do not be deceived; neither fornicators, nor idolaters, nor adulterers, nor effeminate, nor homosexuals, nor thieves, nor the covetous, nor drunkards, nor revilers, nor swindlers, shall inherit the kingdom of God. *And such were some of you; but you were washed, but you were sanctified, but you were justified in the name of the Lord Jesus Christ, and in the Spirit of our God* (1 Corinthians 6:9–11, emphasis added).

FOR THOSE WHO FIND THEMSELVES INTERESTED IN HOMOSEXUALITY

God's Word forbids *desires* that are sinful as well as *deeds* that are sinful. If the Bible prohibits a certain behavior, the longing for or the inclination toward performing such behavior is sinful as well. We are not contending that sins of inclination are the same (or as sinful) as the expression of that inclination into deeds, or homosexual acts. We are, however, asserting the biblical truth that both the desire for that which is sinful and the sinful acts themselves are morally unacceptable. By recognizing a distinction between desire and deed, we have said nothing about the moral acceptability of either. Only God can determine the morality of any particular desire or action. Since God has declared homosexuality to be sinful, it necessarily follows that the desire or the inclination toward homosexuality is sinful as well. To use another example, as God has declared adultery to be contrary to His holiness, even the lusting after or the longing for adultery is forbidden (Matthew 5:28).

What is the responsibility before you if you are struggling with the inordinate lusts of homosexual desire? You must, like Joseph, flee such immorality. Repentance is pleasing to God, yet so many have been told the lie that says change is impossible. Is change possible? Absolutely! (1 Corinthians 6:11). Hope abounds, because homosexuality is sin, and Jesus Christ came to save sinners. That Christian counselors have been unfaithful to the Word of God at this point is a tragedy. All too often they refuse to call homosexuality what it truly is: a violation of God's Word.

Without question, the lusts of homosexual longing can be fierce combatants. "Beloved, I urge you as aliens and strangers to abstain from fleshly lusts which *war against the soul*" (1 Peter 2:11, emphasis added). Romans 1:27 says, "men . . . *burned* in their desire toward one another" (emphasis added). But where sin abounds, grace abounds all the more (Romans 5:20). Those who turn to the Lord Jesus Christ have been given all things that pertain to life and godliness (2 Peter 1:3). Even though many in the church are attempting to justify the practice of homosexuality and are therefore redefining God's standards of holiness, *you* must not. To do so is a soul-damning practice. We must not allow ourselves to be deceived into calling evil good and good evil.

We recognize the biblical distinction between those who teach that God approves of homosexuality and those who are taught these lies. As previously mentioned, the teacher will be held to a higher standard and will incur a stricter judgment (James 3:1; 2 Peter 2). This book has exposed the lies of those who are allowing sin to increase. Do not allow yourself to be led down the path to destruction. Why should you be taken captive by their lies and massive rationalizations? Ask yourself, "What has God said?" His Word is clear. The teaching that is offered by these advocates of immorality has been shown to be contrary to the Bible. Now, what will you do? Will you continue to pursue these sinful lusts?

You may reply that you have no interest in members of the opposite sex. You are not guilty of sin in this regard. You violate no precept of God simply because you do not desire an intimate relationship with a member of the opposite sex. Your sin, in part, is in your discontent with your state as a single person. Even if you truly have no interest in the opposite sex, your status as a single person still prevents you from seeking sexual intimacy of any kind outside of marriage. This teaching may not sound easy to swallow at first, but what does the Scripture clearly tell us? God has prescribed such relations to occur only within the covenant of marriage. All else is adultery or fornication: "Let marriage be held in honor among all, and let the marriage bed be undefiled; for fornicators and adulterers God will judge" (Hebrews 13:4). As we have already seen, marriage is to be between one man and one woman, and this particular passage teaches us that marriage is to be held in honor among all, even among those who must remain in a state of contented singleness for the present.

If you profess to be a disciple of the Lord Jesus Christ, we think you'll agree that you ought to be exhibiting the fruit of the Spirit; you ought to be a person who is exercising self-control in all areas of your life (Galatians 5:23). This requirement is not optional for you if you bear the name of Christ. In this regard, the struggles of a person with homosexual lusts are not at all dissimilar to the struggles of a person with heterosexual lusts. Both must practice self-control. Both must remain celibate unless and until God allows them to marry.

If you are currently married, discipline and self-control are required for you as well. Hebrews 13:4 and 5 are clear: "Fornicators and adulterers God will judge. Let your conduct be free from covetousness" (which is another way to say, "Be content"). Our Lord Jesus Christ denounced the sin of lusting after another so as to commit adultery. One's marriage vows can be broken and the bonds of intimacy that are provided for in marriage can be rejected through the interest in and pursuit of another, even another of the same sex. Many—even among the church—have rejected God's Word on the subject of homosexuality. To renounce one's marriage vows *and* pursue a homosexual relationship is to *compound* sin; this is adding sin upon sin. This is to render one's sinfulness *more* grievous. Some sins are more heinous than other sins. The gravity of a transgression may be considered as greater due to the persons who are sinning (e.g., leaders, pastors), by the persons sinned against (e.g., children, particularly weak persons), or even by the nature of the sin itself (e.g., the multiplication of sins).[3] For those who are married, marriage is God's institution and the disregard of such vows is no simple matter: "It is better that you should not vow than that you should vow and not pay" (Ecclesiastes 5:5).

FOR THOSE WHO ARE CURRENTLY PRACTICING HOMOSEXUALS

Whatever the cause of your behavior, it is nevertheless sinful. The Bible admonishes you to repent of your interests *and* behavior. You must forsake them. Not to put too fine a point on it, these deeds are yours, and you will be held responsible. God will not allow you to blame someone else for your conduct, but, believe it or not, this truth is a source of great hope:

> The fact that homosexual desires and deeds are willful sins for which the person is morally responsible is overwhelmingly important if there is to be any hope in the Christian perspective on homosexuality. When responsibility for homosexuality is removed, hope for homosexuality as an unchangeable inner domination by those drives or desires doom the sinner to despair. And such despair is unnecessary, unwarranted, untrue to Scripture. Because homosexuality is sinful, there is divinely guaranteed hope for its reversal. Christ came to die for sinners and to deliver them by His Spirit from their sins. Not only has our guilt been removed, but also our moral pollution is being set right.[4]

Homosexual *practices* are not unpardonable sins. Forgiveness is possible. Repentance and change are possible. Will you cease to engage in practices that are destructive and condemned by God?

> For if you live according to the flesh you will die; but if by the Spirit you put to death the deeds of the body, you will live. (Romans 8:13 NKJV)

As with homosexual lusts, so too with homosexual practices—the war is on. By this time, you have probably developed a whole host of poor sexual practices. Please accept this frank admonition: It is truly a lazy sexual preference to engage in intimacy with someone *just like* yourself. You may be surprised at this statement, but take a moment to think about it: same-sex partners have the same types of desires, the same types of expectations, and naturally respond in the same way to each other. As one writer phrased it, "Singing in harmony is harder than singing in unison."[5] Once you learn to think God's thoughts after Him, you will begin to hear how much more beautiful the harmony sounds than the monotone voices you are used to, even if you can't fathom it today. Realize that you may not be able to comprehend such music at the moment because you've never heard the notes quite that way before!

In the end, God requires that your practices align themselves with what He desires. God *nowhere and in no way* allows for homosexuality. But the one who repents and turns to Him, though the battle will be intense, will not be forsaken. God promises great blessing to those who forsake a life of sin in order to seek His face (Isaiah 55:6–9). The Bible tells us that He is abounding in compassion and slow to anger, though He is at the same time a consuming fire, jealous for His glory (Exodus 34:6–7; Deuteronomy 4:24; Psalm 103:8–14; 145:8–21; Nahum 1:2–8; Hebrews 12:29). The Lord is loving and holy—a benevolent yet sovereign King. As such, you can soon learn the joy of standing in awe in His presence.

The hallmark of Christ's followers is that they pursue

habits of holiness. You are to "work out your salvation with fear and trembling" (Philippians 2:12) and "discipline yourself for the purpose of godliness" (1 Timothy 4:7).[6] A life with Christ is a life of discipline. C. S. Lewis understood this about Christianity. He wrote, "It is no good asking for a simple religion. After all, real things are not simple."[7] You must train yourself in the school of God's Word—knowing what it teaches and laboring to apply it in your life.

If you have been united with Christ Jesus, you are to make no provision for the lusts of the flesh (Romans 13:14). If you belong to Jesus Christ you shall "not let sin reign in your mortal body that you should obey its lusts." You shall "not go on presenting the members of your body to sin as instruments of unrighteousness; but present yourselves to God as those alive from the dead, and your members as instruments of righteousness to God" (Romans 6:12–13). Remember, though, that such commands come from a perfect and all-knowing God. Since we are created by Him, it follows that we will be most fulfilled when we live in the way in which He created us to live. Augustine stated this well: "Thou hast formed us for Thyself, and our hearts are restless till they find rest in Thee."[8] This world doesn't belong to the fallen culture that wants to claim it; it belongs to the Lord who created heaven *and* earth (Psalm 24:1–6; 50:7–15; Acts 17:24–31). Don't be duped by the lie that worldly ways work best while we're in the world. This is God's world, and His ways work best in it. We were created for His glory; when we glorify Him, we will find our greatest happiness (Psalm 16:7–11; 37:1–6). The *Westminster Larger Catechism* puts it nicely: "Man's chief and highest end is to glorify God, and fully to enjoy him for ever."[9]

To whom do you belong? Do you profess to follow the God of the Bible? If you do, follow His Word and obey His commands: "By this we know that we have come to know Him, if we keep His commandments. The one who says, 'I have come to know Him,' and does not keep His commandments, is a liar, and the truth is not in him" (1 John 2:3–4). God doesn't allow any wiggle room. Both for His glory and for your good, He requires that you forsake homosexual behavior and come to Him in genuine repentance. Be prepared; you will probably lose a number of "friends" who are not true friends in the first place. A true friend—a biblical friend—desires the glory of God before all else and does not seek to encourage you in a lifestyle that is offensive to God and will lead to your hurt. Such a friend would point to the Word of God and show sincere concern for you by bringing to your attention those behaviors and interests that are contrary to God's Word: "Better is open rebuke than love that is concealed. Faithful are the wounds of a friend, but deceitful are the kisses of an enemy" (Proverbs 27:5–6). Never fear faithfulness to God's Word.

Notes

1. David Chilton, *Power in the Blood: A Christian Response to AIDS*, 1987, 116 (out of print).
2. Ibid.
3. See a helpful discussion of the degrees of sinfulness in the *Westminster Larger Catechism*, questions 150 and 151.
4. Greg Bahnsen, *Homosexuality: A Biblical View*, 83.
5. Douglas Wilson, *Fidelity* (Moscow, Ida.: Canon Press, 1999), 105.
6. In 1 Timothy 4:7, the Greek word for *discipline* is *gumnadzo*, from which we obtain our English word *gymnasium*. The follower of Jesus Christ is to discipline himself in such a way with the practices of holiness that it is as if he is in a workout session in the gym.
7. C. S. Lewis, *Mere Christianity* (New York: MacMillan, 1964), 32.
8. *The Confessions of Saint Augustine*, book I, chapter 1, section 1. *The Nicene and Post-Nicene Fathers*, first series, volume 1, 45.
9. *Westminster Larger Catechism* (1648), answer to question 1.

The Relationship of Law and Grace in Romans 6:14

NOT UNDER LAW, BUT UNDER GRACE?

To attempt to evade Leviticus and the clear prohibitions of homosexuality by declaring, "We are not under law, but under grace," is far too simplistic. As we have seen, this phrase is employed in the same-sex controversy in an attempt to reduce the Leviticus prohibitions of homosexuality to irrelevancy. We have also observed that any approach that attempts to dismiss the *entirety* of the book of Leviticus is without biblical warrant. The apostle Paul wrote, "For sin shall not be master over you, for you are not under law, but under grace" (Romans 6:14). An obvious distinction—an *antithesis*—does exist between law and grace, but are they antithetical in such a way that they render the book of Leviticus irrelevant and without bearing in the life of the Christian? How are we to understand these words concerning law and grace? Does the Law have any place in the life of the Christian?

It is clear that Paul did not intend to teach that the Law has absolutely no relevance, bearing, or place in the life of the Christian. Paul taught in the same epistle to the Romans that the Law is not to be discarded, but that it is "established" (3:31). He also taught of the convicting work of the Law—that the Law exposed his sin and revealed his rebellion (7:7–9). Paul referred to the Law as "holy, righteous, and good" (7:12) and that which the spiritual (contrasted to the "fleshly") mind is enabled to pursue and become desirous of pursuing (8:5–7). Most conclusive is that the apostle Paul, teaching about living in a loving way, quoted a portion of the Ten Commandments and then the book of Leviticus. Paul wrote,

> Owe nothing to anyone except to love one another; for he who loves his neighbor has fulfilled the law. For this, "YOU SHALL NOT COMMIT ADULTERY, YOU SHALL NOT MURDER, YOU SHALL NOT STEAL, YOU SHALL NOT COVET," and if there is any other commandment, it is summed up in this saying, "YOU SHALL LOVE YOUR NEIGHBOR AS YOURSELF." Love does no wrong to a neighbor; love therefore is the fulfillment of the law. (13:8–10)

Paul is consistent with the teaching of the whole Bible: the one who loves his neighbor has "fulfilled the law." If the Law is to have no bearing or relevance in the Christian life, Paul would not have referred to the Christian obligation of fulfilling the Law. In demonstrating what Christians owe to one another, Paul cites the Seventh, Sixth, Eighth, and Tenth Commandments and concludes that such conduct toward others can be summed up in the words of Leviticus 19:18: "You shall love your neighbor as yourself."

In the same epistle in which the apostle Paul taught that "We are not under law, but under grace," he also demonstratively teaches us that the Law is valid for the Christian. Paul must have meant something *other* than to say that the Law is irrelevant and not applicable when he wrote that we are not "under law, but under grace."

We find the same in other writings of the apostle. Paul wrote in 1 Corinthians, "Circumcision is nothing, and uncircumcision is nothing, but what matters is the keeping of the commandments of God" (7:19). While encouraging the Corinthian church to live in accordance with holiness, Paul again quoted from Leviticus: "I will dwell in them and walk among them; and I will be their God, and they shall be My people" (2 Corinthians 6:16; Leviticus 26:12). Paul consistently quoted the Old Testament as authoritative for the New Testament era. He did this in matters of supporting the work of the ministry (1 Corinthians 9:9; 1 Timothy 5:18) as well as in matters of accepting accusations against others (2 Corinthians 13:1; 1 Timothy 5:20). Paul again quoted from Leviticus 19:18 in Galatians 5:14 and cited the Fifth Commandment in

Ephesians 6:2. The Law of God was relevant and authoritative for the apostle Paul.

To clarify, however, some portions of the Old Testament law are, in fact, no longer binding, particularly the ceremonial law. Paul clearly refers to these aspects of the Law as no longer obligatory (1 Corinthians 7:19; Ephesians 2:11–22; Colossians 2:16–17). Furthermore, he is clear that the Law was never intended to justify sinful man: "For if righteousness comes through the Law, then Christ died needlessly" (Galatians 2:21; see also Galatians 3:21; 5:4; Romans 3:28). Salvation has always been by grace and through faith, never due to the works of the Law (Romans 4:1–13; Galatians 3:6–9; Ephesians 2:8–9; Hebrews 11). Paul never presents the Law as something that justifies. Paul does, however, speak of obedience to the commands of God as evidence of already being justified.

The Lord Jesus Christ taught this truth as well. Obedience to the commands of God is evidence of Christian discipleship. Obedience to the commands of God does not *make* one a disciple, but obedience reveals the new heart, a heart that has been enabled to obey. John Murray explained this point and illustrated the confusion present in many churches. He wrote,

> It is symptomatic of a pattern of thought current in many evangelical circles that the idea of keeping the commandments of God is not consonant with the liberty and spontaneity of the Christian man, that *keeping* the law has its affinities with legalism and with the principle of works rather than with the principle of grace. It is

strange indeed that this kind of antipathy to the notion of keeping commandments should be entertained by any believer who is a serious student of the New Testament. Did not our Lord say, "If ye love me, ye will keep my commandments" (John 14:15)? And did he not say, "If ye keep my commandments, ye shall abide in my love, even as I have kept my Father's commandments and abide in his love" (John 15:10)?[1]

Murray continues this line of reasoning, this time calling upon John, the disciple whom Jesus loved.

It was John who recorded these sayings of our Lord and it was he, of all the disciples, who was mindful of the Lord's teaching and example regarding love, and reproduces that teaching so conspicuously in his first Epistle. We catch something of the tenderness of his entreaty when he writes, "Little children, let us not love in word, neither in tongue, but in deed and truth" (1 John 3:18). "Beloved, let us love one another, for love is of God" (1 John 4:7). But the message of John has escaped us if we have failed to note John's emphasis upon the keeping of the commandments of God. "And by this we know that we know him, if we keep his commandments. He that says, I know him, and does not keep his commandments, is a liar, and the truth is not in him. But whoso keeps his word, in him verily the love of God is made perfect" (1 John 2:3–5). "Beloved, if our heart does not condemn, we have confidence toward God, and whatsoever we ask we receive from him, because we keep his commandments and do those things that are pleasing in his sight ... and he who keeps his commandments abides in him and he in him" (1 John 3:21, 22, 24). "For this is the love of God, that we keep his command-ments" (1 John 5:3).[2]

Murray recognizes, from the biblical passages, that in order for one to be loving one must follow the commands of God. Love is clearly defined by God. Murray drew the following conclusion:

> To say the very least, the witness of our Lord and the testimony of John are to the effect that there is indispen-sable complementation; love will be operative in the *keeping* of God's commandments. It is only myopia that prevents us from seeing this, and when there is a persist-ent animosity to the notion of keeping commandments, the only conclusion is that there is either gross igno-rance or malignant opposition to the testimony of Jesus.[3]

It is clear the apostle Paul did not mean that we are under *no* obligation to obey the commands of God when he wrote that we are not under law, but under grace. So, what do these words mean? In Romans 6, Paul is teaching about what it means to be united with Jesus Christ. Those who have been united with Christ, those who are in union with Christ, now live a new life—they walk "in newness of life" (6:4). Those who are in union with Jesus Christ do not "continue in sin so that grace may abound" (6:1), they should "no longer be slaves to sin" (6:6). This implies that previously, prior to being united with Christ, they had been slaves to sin but now they are under a new master: they are to be slaves of righteousness (6:19–20).

Previously, they were under the dominion and the condemnation of the Law (they were guilty) because they were slaves of sin. The Law stood over them in condemnation; they were "under Law." But now, they are given new life, they are "under grace," they have a new master, they are "enslaved to God" (6:22).

A strong contrast, an antithesis, exists between enslavement to sin and enslavement to righteousness. Slaves have masters, and Romans 6:14 explains, "For sin shall not be *master* over you, for you are not under law, but under grace." Previously, before being enslaved to God and righteousness, those who are now believers lived in utter violation of the Law "just as you presented your members as slaves to impurity and to lawlessness, resulting in further lawlessness" (6:19). As transgressors, they were "under the law," that is, they were under the judgment of the Law. But now, those who are under grace are no longer under the dominion of the Law. They are no longer under the judgment and condemnation of the Law; they are under grace and show themselves to be slaves of righteousness (6:19). To state the matter simply, those who are united to Christ are no longer under *judgment*, they are under *justification*.

Christians, those people united to Jesus Christ, are not under the Law, they are under grace. Those who are under grace no longer submit, in habitual fashion, their bodies to impurity and lawlessness. Those who are under grace submit themselves to lawfulness, to righteousness—they submit themselves to the clear teaching of God's

Word, even in Leviticus. Properly understood, Romans 6:14 offers no support for those who are trying to justify their homosexual desires and practice; therefore, we must conclude that the Law of God has bearing, relevance, and authority in the life of the New Testament saint.

Notes

1. John Murray, *Principles of Conduct: Aspects of Biblical Ethics* (Grand Rapids: Eerdmans, 1991), 182–83.
2. Ibid., 183.
3. Ibid.

John Chrysostom (347-407) on Romans 1[1]

THE HOMILIES ON THE EPISTLE OF ST. PAUL THE APOSTLE TO THE ROMANS

Homily 4 on Romans 1:26–27

"For this cause God gave them up unto vile affections: for even their women did change the natural use into that which is against nature: and likewise also the men, leaving the natural use of the woman, burned in their lust one towards another."

ALL these affections then were vile, but chiefly the mad lust after males; for the soul is more the sufferer in sins, and more dishonored, than the body in diseases. But behold how here too, as in the case of the doctrines, he deprives them of excuse, by saying of the women, that "they changed the natural use." For no one, he means, can say that it was by being hindered of legitimate intercourse that they came to this pass, or that it was from having no means to fulfill their desire that they were driven into this monstrous insaneness. For the changing implies possession. Which also when discoursing upon the doctrines he said, "They changed the truth of God for a lie." And with regard to the men again, he shows the same thing by saying, "Leaving the natural use of the woman." And in a like way with those, these he also puts out of all means of defending themselves by charging them not only that they had the means of gratification, and left that which they had, and went after another, but that having dishonored that which was natural, they ran after that which was contrary to nature. But that which is contrary to nature hath in it an irksomeness and displeasingness, so that they could not fairly allege even pleasure. For genuine pleasure is that which is according to nature. But when God hath left one, then all things are turned upside down. And thus not only was their doctrine Satanical, but their life too was diabolical.

Now when he was discoursing of their doctrines, he put before them the world and man's understanding, telling them that, by the judgment afforded them by God, they might through the things which are seen, have been led as by the hand to the Creator, and then by not willing to do so, they remained inexcusable. Here in the place of the world he sets the pleasure according to nature, which they would have enjoyed with more sense of security and greater glad-heartedness, and so have been far removed from shameful deeds. But they would not; whence they are quite out of the pale of pardon, and have done an insult to nature itself. And a yet more disgraceful thing than these is it, when even the women seek after these intercourses, who ought to have more sense of shame than men.

And here too the judgment of Paul is worthy of admiration, how having fallen upon two opposite matters he accomplishes them both with all exactness. For he wished both to speak chastely and to sting the hearer. Now both these things were not in his power to do, but one hindered the other. For if you speak chastely you shall not be able to bear hard upon the hearer. But if you are minded to touch him to the quick, you are forced to lay the naked facts before him in plain terms. But his discreet and holy soul was able to do both with exactness, and by naming nature has at once given additional force to his accusation, and also used this as a sort of veil, to keep the chasteness of his description. And next, having reproached the women first, he goes on to the men also, and says, "And likewise also the men leaving the natural use of the woman." Which is an evident proof of the last degree of corruptness, when both sexes are abandoned, and both he that was ordained to be the instructor of the woman, and she who was bid to become an helpmate to the man, work the deeds of enemies against one another.

And reflect too how significantly he uses his words. For he does not say that they were enamored of, and lusted after one another, but, "they burned in their lust one toward another." You see that the whole of desire comes of an exorbitancy which endureth not to abide within its proper limits. For everything which transgresseth the laws by God appointed, lusteth after monstrous things and not those which be customary. For as many oftentimes having left the desire of food get to feed upon earth and small stones, and others being possessed by excessive thirst often long even for mire, thus these also ran into this ebullition of lawless love. But if you say, and whence came this intensity of lust? It was from the desertion of God: and whence is the desertion of God? from the lawlessness of them that left Him; "men with men working that which is unseemly." Do not, he means, because you have heard that they burned, suppose that the evil was only in desire. For the greater part of it came of their luxuriousness, which also kindled into flame their lust. And this is why he did not say being swept along or being overtaken, an expression he uses elsewhere, but what? working. They made a business of the sin, and not only a business, but even one zealously followed up. And he called it not lust, but that which is unseemly, and that properly? For they both dishonored nature, and trampled on the laws.

And see the great confusion which fell out on both sides. For not only was the head turned downwards but the feet too were upwards, and they became enemies to themselves and to one another, bringing in a pernicious kind of strife, and one even more lawless than any civil war, and one rife in divisions, and of varied form. For they divided this into four new, and lawless kinds. Since (3 Mss. whence) this war was not twofold or threefold, but even fourfold. Consider then. It was meet, that the twain should be one, I mean the woman and the man. For "the twain," it says, "shall be one flesh." (Genesis 2:24.) But this the desire of intercourse effected, and united the sexes to one another. This desire the devil having taken away, and having turned the course thereof into another fashion, he thus sundered the sexes from one another, and made the one to become two parts in opposition to the law of God. For it says, "the two shall be one flesh;" but he divided the one flesh into two: here then is one war. Again, these same two parts he provoked to war both against themselves and against one another. For even women again abused women, and not men only. And the men stood against one another, and against the female sex, as happens in a battle by night. You see a second and third war, and a fourth and fifth; there is also another, for beside what have been mentioned they also behaved lawlessly against nature itself. For when the Devil saw that this desire is, principally, which draws the sexes together, he was bent on cutting through the tie, so as to destroy the race, not only by their not copulating lawfully, but also by their being stirred up to war, and in sedition against one another.

"And receiving in themselves that recompense of their error which was meet." See how he goes again to the fountainhead of the evil, namely, the impiety that comes of their doctrines, and this he says is a reward of that lawlessness. For since in speaking of hell and punishment, it seemed he would not at present be credible to the ungodly and deliberate choosers of such a life, but even scorned, he shows that the punishment was in this pleasure itself. (So Plato *Theaet.* 176, 7.) But if they perceive it not, but are still pleased, be not amazed. For even they that are mad, and are afflicted with frenzy (cf. Soph. *Aj.* 265–77) while doing themselves much injury and making themselves such objects of compassion, that others weep over them themselves, smile and revel over what has happened.

Yet we do not only for this not say that they are quit of punishment, but for this very reason are under a more grievous vengeance, in that they are unconscious of the plight they are in. For it is not the disordered but those who are sound whose votes one has to gain. Yet of old the matter seemed even to be a law, and a certain law-giver among them bade the domestic slaves neither to use unguents when dry (i.e. except in bathing) nor to keep youths, giving the free this place of honor, or rather of shamefulness. Yet they, however, did not think the thing shameful, but as being a grand privilege, and one too great for slaves, the Athenian people, the wisest of people, and Solon who is so great amongst them, permitted it to the free alone. And sundry other books of the philosophers may one see full of this disease. But we do not therefore say that the thing was made lawful, but that they who received this law were pitiable, and objects for many tears.

For these are treated in the same way as women that play the whore. Or rather their plight is more miserable. For in the case of the one the intercourse, even if lawless, is yet according to nature: but this is contrary both to law and nature. For even if there were no hell, and no punishment had been threatened, this were worse than any punishment. Yet if you say "they found pleasure in it," you tell me what adds to the vengeance. For suppose I were to see a person running naked, with his body all besmeared with mire, and yet not covering himself, but exulting in it, I should not rejoice with him, but should rather bewail that he did not even perceive that he was doing shamefully. But that I may show the atrocity in a yet clearer light, bear with me in one more example.

Now if any one condemned a virgin to live in close dens (θαλομευομένην), and to have intercourse with unreasoning brutes, and then she was pleased with such intercourse, would she not for this be especially a worthy object of tears, as being unable to be freed from this misery owing to her not even perceiving the misery? It is plain surely to every one. But if that were a grievous thing, neither is this less so than that. For to be insulted by one's own kinsmen is more piteous than to be so by strangers: these I say (5 Mss. "I consider") are even worse than murderers: since to die even is better than to live under such insolency. For the murderer dissevers the soul from the body, but this man ruins the soul with the body. And name what sin you will, none will you mention equal to this lawlessness. And if they that suffer such things perceived them, they would accept ten thousand deaths so they might not suffer this evil. For there is not, there surely is not, a more grievous evil than this insolent dealing. For if when discoursing about fornication Paul said, that "Every sin which a man doeth is without the body, but he that committeth fornication sinneth against his own body" (1 Corinthians 6:18); what shall we say of this madness, which is so much worse than fornication as cannot even be expressed?

For I should not only say that thou hast become a woman, but that thou hast lost thy manhood, and hast neither changed into that nature nor kept that which thou haddest, but thou hast been a traitor to both of them at once, and deserving both of men and women to be driven out and stoned, as having wronged either sex. And that thou mayest learn what the real force of this is, if any one were to come and assure you that he would make you a dog instead of being a man, would you not flee from him as a plague? But, lo! thou hast not made thyself a dog out of a man, but an animal more disgraceful than this. For this is useful unto service, but he that hath thus given himself up is serviceable for nothing.

Or again, if any one threatened to make men travail and be brought to bed, should we not be filled with indignation? But lo! now they that have run into this fury have done more grievously by themselves. For it is not the same thing to change into the nature of women, as to continue a man and yet to have become a woman; or rather neither this nor that. But if you would know the enormity of the evil from other grounds, ask on what account the law-givers punish them that make men eunuchs, and you will see that it is absolutely for no other reason than because they mutilate nature. And yet the injustice they do is nothing to this. For there have been those that were mutilated and were in many cases useful after their mutilation. But nothing can there be more worthless than a man who has pandered himself. For not the soul only, but the body also of one who hath been so treated, is disgraced, and deserves to be driven out everywhere. How many hells shall be enough for such?

But if thou scoffest at hearing of hell and believest not that fire, remember Sodom. For we have seen, surely we have seen, even in this present life, a semblance of hell. For since many would utterly disbelieve the things to come after the resurrection, hearing now of an unquenchable fire, God brings them to a right mind by things present. For such is the burning of Sodom, and that conflagration! And they know it well that have been at the place, and have seen with their eyes that scourge divinely sent, and the effect of the lightnings from above. (Jude 7) Consider how great is that sin, to have forced hell to appear even before its time! For whereas many thought scorn of His words, by His deeds did God show them the image thereof in a certain novel way. For that rain was unwonted, for that the intercourse was contrary to nature, and it deluged the land, since lust had done so with their souls. Wherefore also the rain was the opposite of the customary rain. Now not only did it fail to stir up the womb of the earth to the production of fruits, but made it even useless for the reception of seed. For such was also the intercourse of the men, making a body of this sort more worthless than the very land of Sodom.

And what is there more detestable than a man who hath pandered himself, or what more execrable? Oh, what madness! Oh, what distraction! Whence came this lust lewdly reveling and making man's nature all that enemies could? or even worse than that, by as much as the soul is better than the body. Oh, ye that were more senseless than irrational creatures, and more shameless than dogs! for in no case does such intercourse take place with them, but nature acknowledgeth her own limits. But ye have even made our race dishonored below things irrational, by such indignities inflicted upon and by each other. Whence then were these evils born? Of luxury; of not knowing God. For so soon as any have cast out the fear of Him, all that is good straightway goes to ruin.

Now, that this may not happen, let us keep clear before our eyes the fear of God. For nothing, surely nothing, so ruins a man as to slip from this anchor, as nothing saves so much as continually looking thereto. For if by having a man before our eyes we feel more backward at doing sins, and often even through feeling abashed at servants of a better stamp we keep from doing anything amiss, consider what safety we shall enjoy by having God before our eyes! For in no case will the Devil attack us when so conditioned, in that he would be laboring without profit.

But should he see us wandering abroad, and going

about without a bridle, by getting a beginning ourselves he will be able to drive us off afterwards any whither. And as it happens with thoughtless servants at market, who leave the needful services which their masters have entrusted to them, and rivet themselves at a mere haphazard to those who fall in their way, and waste out their leisure there; this also we undergo when we depart from the commandments of God. For we presently get standing on, admiring riches, and beauty of person, and the other things which we have no business with, just as those servants attend to the beggars that do jugglers' feats, and then, arriving too late, have to be grievously beaten at home. And many pass the road set before them through following others, who are behaving in the same unseemly way.

But let not us so do. For we have been sent to dispatch many affairs that are urgent. And if we leave those, and stand gaping at these useless things, all our time will be wasted in vain and to no profit, and we shall suffer the extreme of punishment. For if you wish yourself to be busy, you have whereat you ought to wonder, and to gape all your days, things which are no subject for laughter, but for wondering and manifold praises. As he that admires things ridiculous, will himself often be such, and even worse than he that occasioneth the laughter. And that you may not fall into this, spring away from it forthwith.

For why is it, pray, that you stand gaping and fluttering at the sight of riches? What do you see so wonderful, and able to fix your eyes upon them? These gold-harnessed horses, these lackeys, partly savages, and partly eunuchs, and costly raiment, and the soul that is getting utterly soft in all this, and the haughty brow, and the bustlings, and the noise? And wherein do these things deserve wonder? What are they better than the beggars that dance and pipe in the market-place? For these too being taken with a sore famine of virtue, dance a dance more ridiculous than theirs, led and carried round at one time to costly tables, at another to the lodging of prostitute women, and at another to a swarm of flatterers and a host of hangers-on. But if they do wear gold, this is why they are the most pitiable, because the things which are nothing to them, are most the subject of their eager desire. Do not now, I pray, look at their raiment, but open their soul, and consider if it is not full of countless wounds, and clad with rags, and destitute, and defenseless!

What then is the use of this madness of shows? For it were much better to be poor and living in virtue, than to be a king with wickedness; since the poor man in himself enjoys all the delights of the soul, and doth not even perceive his outward poverty for his inward riches. But the king, luxurious in those things which do not at all belong to him, is punished in those things which are his most real concern, even the soul, the thoughts, and the conscience, which are to go away with him to the other world. Since then we know these things, let us lay aside the gilded raiment, let us take up virtue and the pleasure which comes thereof. For so, both here and hereafter, shall we come to enjoy great delights, through the grace and love towards man of our Lord Jesus Christ, through Whom, and with Whom, be glory to the Father, with the Holy Spirit, for ever and ever. Amen.

Notes

1. *The Nicene and Post-Nicene Fathers*, Chrysostom: *The Epistle to the Romans*, volume 11, 355–59.

Homosexuality As an Abomination: Moral or Ceremonial Uncleanness?

> You shall not lie with a male as one lies with a female; it is an *abomination*. (Leviticus 18:22)
>
> If there is a man who lies with a male as those who lie with a woman, both of them have committed a *detestable act*; they shall surely be put to death. Their blood-guiltiness is upon them. (Leviticus 20:13) (emphasis added)

Leviticus 18:22 and 20:13 refer to homosexuality as an abomination, a detestable act. Both passages use the Hebrew word *toevah*, and the context demands that the word be understood as referring to that which is morally unacceptable to God. However, revisionists who contend that the Bible does not prohibit all forms of homosexuality, declare that the word *toevah* actually refers to some manner of ritual or religious uncleanness and not moral defilement; they argue that the word speaks *solely* of ceremonial defilement.

By choosing such a definition, without regard to the context, however, the revisionists unwittingly reveal some level of recognition between the moral and ceremonial aspects of God's law. In order to dismiss Leviticus from the current discussion on homosexuality, they vigorously strive to place the prohibitions of Leviticus against the practice into the ceremonial category, thus reducing them to an exclusively Jewish issue.[1] Late homosexual author John Boswell represented this viewpoint.

> The Hebrew word *toevah*, here translated "abomination," does not usually signify something intrinsically evil, like rape or theft (discussed elsewhere in Leviticus), but something which is ritually unclean for Jews, like eating pork or engaging in intercourse during menstruation, both of which are prohibited in these same chapters. It is used throughout the Old Testament to designate those Jewish sins which involve ethnic contamination or idolatry and very frequently occurs as part of the stock phrase *toevah ha-goyim*, "the uncleanness of the Gentiles" (e.g., 2 Kings 16:3).
>
> Chapter 20 begins with a prohibition of sexual idolatry almost identical with this, and like 18, its manifest (and stated: 20:3–4) purpose is to elaborate a system of ritual "cleanliness" whereby the Jews will be distinguished from neighboring peoples. Although both chapters also contain prohibitions (e.g., against incest and

adultery) that would seem to stem from moral absolutes, their function in the context of Leviticus 18 and 20 seems to be as symbols of Jewish distinctiveness.

In the Greek, then, the Levitical enactments against homosexual behavior characterize it unequivocally as ceremonially unclean rather than inherently evil.[2]

More recently, Roman Catholic priest Daniel Helminiak commented similarly.

> "Abomination" is a translation of the word *toevah.* This term could also be translated "uncleanness" or "impurity" or "dirtiness." "Taboo," what is culturally or ritually forbidden, would be another accurate translation.
>
> The significance of the term *toevah* becomes clear when you realize that another Hebrew term *zimah* could have been used—if that was what the authors intended. *Zimah* means, not what is objectionable for religious or cultural reasons, but what is wrong in itself. It means an injustice, a sin.
>
> Clearly, then, Leviticus does not say that for man to lie with man is a sin. Leviticus says it is a ritual violation, an uncleanness; it is something "dirty."[3]

Such revisionist authors assert that *toevah* (abomination) does not refer to something that is "inherently" or "intrinsically evil, like rape or theft." They want us to believe that *toevah* does not refer to that which is morally wrong; it is merely referring to some type of ritual uncleanness, a ceremonial impurity. Helminiak goes so far as to liken the usage of the word *toevah* to social indiscretions such as "picking one's nose, burping, or passing gas,"[4] showing himself to be guilty, either blindly or purposefully, of the malpractice in translation of designating such things as abominable when the Bible does not do so. The only way these revisionists can maintain their assertion that the Leviticus prohibitions of homosexuality are an exclusively Jewish (ceremonial) matter, something that pertained only to the Jewish religious and cultural environment of that day, is if their translation and interpretation of Leviticus is valid.

RELATIVISM AND INCONSISTENCY
IN INTERPRETATION

Boswell revealed a blatant moral relativism in his struggle with the presence of adultery and incest in Leviticus 18 and 20. He wrote, "Although both chapters also contain prohibitions [e.g., against incest and adultery] which would seem to stem from moral absolutes, their function in the context of Leviticus 18 and 20 seems to be as symbols of Jewish distinctiveness." Boswell *must* categorize these prohibitions as "symbols of Jewish distinctiveness" (forcing them to fit into his cubbyhole of ritual impurity) or else his entire argument fails. To admit that incest or adultery in this context is "inherently" or "intrinsically evil" would be to admit the presence of non-ritual uncleanness, which is described as *toevah.*

Boswell evidenced inconsistency as well. A simple study of the word *toevah* reveals an insurmountable obstacle for his interpretation. Numerous times in the Hebrew Bible we find that the word *toevah* refers to *the sins that were committed by the pagan nations surrounding Israel.* Now, if *toevah* is to be restricted to Jewish (ceremonial, ritual) uncleanness, and if it exhibited some type of "Jewish distinctiveness," then the word should not be able to be applied to those outside of Israel; such a usage would not make any sense. The revisionists tell us that the sins described as *toevah* refer to those things that are exclusively Jewish: the dietary laws, the regulations against the mixing of cattle, seed, and fabrics, etc. Scripture is clear, though, that the nations surrounding Israel were *never* required to practice these things; it was not *toevah* for them to disregard such rules; however, the Bible does refer to the *sins* of the surrounding nations as *toevah.* A few examples should suffice:

> When you enter the land which the LORD your God gives you, you shall not learn to imitate the detestable things (*toevah*) of those nations. (Deuteronomy 18:9)
>
> ... in order that they may not teach you to do according to all their detestable things (*toevah*) which they have done for their gods, so that you would sin against the LORD your God. (Deuteronomy 20:18)
>
> But he walked in the way of the kings of Israel, and even made his son pass through the fire, according to the abominations (*toevah*) of the nations whom the

LORD had driven out from before the sons of Israel. (2 Kings 16:3)

And he did evil in the sight of the LORD, according to the abominations (*toevah*) of the nations whom the LORD dispossessed before the sons of Israel. (2 Kings 21:2)

Furthermore, all the officials of the priests and the people were very unfaithful following all the abominations (*toevah*) of the nations; and they defiled the house of the LORD which He had sanctified in Jerusalem. (2 Chronicles 36:14)

These verses illustrate the very same facts that we noticed in our consideration of Leviticus 18. The nations that dwelled in the land prior to the Hebrews were judged, driven from the land due to the abominations (*toevah*) that they had committed (see Leviticus 18:24–30). The suggestion that *toevah* refers exclusively to ceremonial or ritual impurity is simply not biblical, since the nations surrounding Israel did not have the ceremonies and rituals to disobey.

Boswell writes that adultery and incest "seem to stem from moral absolutes." They "seem to" because they do. Adultery and incest are sinful because God declares them sinful. Furthermore, they are sinful for all nations, not just the Hebrews. Adultery is referred to as *toevah* elsewhere in the Bible, outside of the Leviticus context. Boswell and similar revisionist interpreters of the book of Leviticus are sold on their idea that the *entire context* of Leviticus is religious and ritual, so let us take a look at *toevah* outside of

Leviticus. Consider Jeremiah 7:9–10:

> Will you steal, murder, and commit adultery, and
> swear falsely, and offer sacrifices to Baal, and walk after
> other gods that you have not known, then come and
> stand before Me in this house, which is called by My
> name, and say, "We are delivered!"—that you may do all
> these abominations?

Stealing, murder, adultery, swearing falsely, idolatry,
and hypocrisy are all described as *toevah* (abominations).
Should these references be reduced to mere social indiscretions or to something improper *only* for the Jews?
Surely not. These practices are sinful, and they are abominations. They are not considered sinful because of the
people or the place; they were sinful and abominable then
and now. The context of the sin is irrelevant. It does not
matter if the arena of such sinful practices is religious or
secular; if it is morally evil, it remains morally evil. Clearly,
the attempted revision of the word *toevah* to refer to something ceremonial or ritual, thus rendering it exclusively an
ancient Jewish matter, fails miserably.[5]

While *toevah* clearly refers to moral evil, the word certainly can refer also to that which is ceremonially unacceptable; however, as we have seen, the fact that the word
can have this application does not mean it is the *exclusive*
application. People can and should accurately understand
that ceremonial or ritual violations of God's law are
described by portions of Scripture as *toevah* because the
rejection of them—disobedience by the covenant people

of the Lord—is tantamount to a rejection of the people's identity as those who belong to the Lord and the obligations they have been given by Him. As well as pointing to the coming Messiah, the ceremonies also identified the people of the Lord; their practices were the practices of those who belong to Jehovah. Rejecting, disregarding, or violating the ceremonies was a way of rejecting the Lord and the worship of Him, and such rebellion declared the people's desire to be like the other nations. *Toevah* is accurately applied to such sins, because the word *cannot* be restricted to ritual, Jewish uncleanness, and does refer to the sins of the nations that surrounded Israel.

Notes

1. See chapters 3, 4, and 5 of this book.
2. *Christianity, Social Tolerance, and Homosexuality,* 100–02.
3. *What the Bible Really Says About Homosexuality,* 64.
4. Ibid., 66.
5. See also Ezekiel 22:11. It is assumed people recognize adultery and incest, which Ezekiel describes as *toevah,* to be immoral for all people and not only Jews.

Augustine (354-430) on Romans 1: Sin and the Penalty of Sin the Same[1]

THE MERITS AND FORGIVENESS OF SINS

A Portion of Augustine's Comments on Romans 1

"The very matter," says [Paul], "of sin is its punishment, if the sinner is so much weakened that he commits more sins." He does not consider how justly the light of truth forsakes the man who transgresses the law. When thus deserted he of course becomes blinded, and necessarily offends more; and by so falling is embarrassed and being embarrassed fails to rise, so as to hear the voice of the law, which admonishes him to beg for the Savior's grace. Is no punishment due to them of whom the apostle says: "Because that, when they knew God, they glorified Him not as God, neither were thankful; but became vain in their imaginations, and their foolish heart was darkened?" This darkening was, of course, already their punishment and penalty; and yet by this very penalty—that is, by their blindness of heart, which supervenes on the withdrawal of the light of wisdom—they fell into more grievous sins still. "For giving themselves out as wise, they became fools."

This is a grievous penalty, if one only understands it; and from such a penalty only see to what lengths they ran: "And they changed," he says, "the glory of the incorruptible God into an image made like to corruptible man, and to birds, and four-footed beasts, and creeping things." All this they did owing to that penalty of their sin, whereby "their foolish heart was darkened." And yet, owing to these deeds of theirs, which, although coming in the way of punishment, were none the less sins (he goes on to say): "Wherefore God also gave them up to uncleanness, through the lusts of their own hearts." See how severely God condemned them, giving them over to uncleanness in the very desires of their heart.

Observe also the sins they commit owing to such condemnation: "To dishonor," says he, "their own bodies among themselves." Here is the punishment of iniquity, which is itself iniquity; a fact which sets forth in a clearer light the words which follow: "Who changed the truth of God into a lie, and worshipped and served the creature more than the Creator, who is blessed for ever. Amen." "For this cause," says he, "God gave them up unto vile

affections." See how often God inflicts punishment; and
out of the self-same punishment sins, more numerous
and more severe, arise. "For even their women did
change the natural use into that which is against nature;
and likewise the men also, leaving the natural use of the
woman, burned in their lust one toward another; men
with men working that which is unseemly." Then, to
show that these things were so sins themselves that they
were also the penalties of sins, he further says: "And
receiving in themselves that recompense of their error
which was meet." Observe how often it happens that the
very punishment which God inflicts begets other sins as
its natural offspring.

Attend still further: "And even as they did not like to
retain God in their knowledge," says he, "God gave them
over to a reprobate mind, to do those things which are not
convenient; being filled with all unrighteousness, fornication, wickedness, covetousness, maliciousness; full of envy,
murder, debate, deceit, malignity; whisperers, backbiters,
odious to God, despiteful, proud, boasters, inventors of
evil things, disobedient to parents, without understanding,
covenant-breakers, without natural affection, implacable,
unmerciful." Here, now, let our opponent say: "Sin ought
not so to have been punished, that the sinner, through his
punishment, should commit even more sins."

Notes

1. *The Nicene and Post-Nicene Fathers,* volume 5: Augustin's Anti-Pelagian Works: *The Merits and Forgiveness of Sins and On the Baptism of Infants—"Sin and the Penalty of Sin the Same,"* book 3, chapter 24 [xxii], 129.

Bibliography

The Ante-Nicene Fathers, volume 2, Fathers of the Second Century: Athenagorus.

The Ante-Nicene Fathers, volume 3, Tertullian, *The Chaplet, or De Corona.*

The Ante-Nicene Fathers, volume 4; Origen, *Against Celsus*, book 7.

The Ante-Nicene Fathers, volume 5; Cyprian, *The Treatises of Cyprian—"Of the Discipline and Advantage of Chastity."*

The Ante-Nicene Fathers, volume 7; Fathers of the Third and Fourth Centuries: Lactantius, *The Divine Institutes*, book 1, chapter 11, 20. *Of the Manner in Which the Persecutors Died*, volume 7.

Bahnsen, Greg L., *Homosexuality: A Biblical View* (Grand Rapids: Baker Book House, 1991).

Bauer, Arndt, Gingrich, and Danker, *A Greek-English Lexicon of the New Testament and Other Early Christian Literature*, (University of Chicago, 1979).

Blair, Ralph, *An Evangelical Look at Homosexuality.*

Boswell, John, *Christianity, Social Tolerance, and Homosexuality* (Chicago: University of Chicago Press, 1980).

"Charlie Coppinger's Side of the 'Gay Chaplain' Story," *Active Christian News*, Dec. 2000.

Chilton, David, *Power in the Blood: A Christian Response to AIDS*, 1987 (out of print).

Clement of Rome, *Epistle to the Corinthians* (*The Apostolic Fathers*).

Colquhoun, John, *A Treatise on the Law and the Gospel,* First American Edition, 1835, reprinted by Soli Deo Gloria, 1999.

Confessions of Saint Augustine, The, book I, chapter 1, section 1. *The Nicene and Post-Nicene Fathers,* first series, volume 1.

Countryman, L. William, *Dirt, Greed, and Sex: Sexual Ethics in the New Testament and Their Implications for Today* (Minneapolis: Augsburg Fortress, 1988).

DeYoung, James B., *Homosexuality: Contemporary Claims Examined in the Light of the Bible and Other Ancient Literature and Law* (Grand Rapids: Kregel, 2000), Excursus Three.

"Does the Bible Prohibit Homosexuality?" *Bible Review,* December 1993.

Einwechter, William, *Ethics and God's Law: An Introduction to Theonomy* (Mill Hall, Penn.: Preston/Speed, 1995).

Gagnon, Robert, *The Bible and Homosexual Practice* (Nashville: Abingdon, 2001).

Geneva Bible of 1560.

Grant, George, and Mark Horne, *Unnatural Affections: The Impuritan Ethic of Homosexuality and the Modern Church* (Nashville: Legacy Press, 1991).

Helminiak, Daniel, *What the Bible Really Says About Homosexuality* (San Francisco: Alamo Square Press, 1995).

Horner, Tom, *Jonathan Loved David: Homosexuality in Biblical Times* (Philadelphia: Westminster Press, 1978).

Irenaeus, *Against Heresies* (*The Ante-Nicene Fathers,* volume 1).

Josephus, *Antiquities of the Jews,* Book 1, XI.1. (*Antiquities,* Book 1).

———. *Wars of the Jews,* Book IV.8.4.

Kaiser, Walter C., *Toward an Old Testament Theology* (Grand Rapids: Zondervan, 1978).

Koop, C. Everett, and Francis Schaeffer, *Whatever Happened to the Human Race,* revised edition (Wheaton, Ill.: Crossway Books, 1983).

Lewis, C. S., *Mere Christianity* (New York: MacMillan, 1964).

London Baptist Confession of 1689.

Malick, David E., "The Condemnation of Homosexuality in 1 Corinthians 6:9," *Bibliotheca Sacra* 150 (October-December, 1993).

McNeill, John J., *The Church and the Homosexual* (Boston: Beacon Press, 1993).

Murray, John, *Principles of Conduct: Aspects of Biblical Ethics* (Grand Rapids: Eerdmans, 1991).

The Nicene and Post-Nicene Fathers, second series, volume 1; Church History of Eusebius: "The Oration of Eusebius Pamphilus, in Praise of the Emperor Constantine."

The Nicene and Post-Nicene Fathers, second series, volume 4; Athanasius: *Select Writings and Letters.*

The Nicene and Post-Nicene Fathers, volume 5; Augustin's Anti-Pelagian Works: *The Merits and Forgiveness of Sins and On the Baptism of Infants—"Sin and the Penalty of Sin the Same," On Marriage and Concupiscence—"He Answers the Arguments of Julianus," What Is the Natural Use of the Woman? What Is the Unnatural Use?*

The Nicene and Post-Nicene Fathers, volume 11; Chrysostom: *Homilies on the Acts of the Apostles and the Epistle to the Romans—Homily 4 on Romans 1:26–27.*

The Nicene and Post-Nicene Fathers, volume 12; Chrysostom: *Homilies on the Epistles of Paul to the Corinthians—Homily 26 on 1 Corinthians 11:2 (verse 15).*

Pattison Fred L., *But Leviticus Says!* (Phoenix: Cristo Press, 1993), 8–9.

Pearson, Dr. Joseph A., video series, *Christianity and Homosexuality (Reconciled).*

Scanzoni, Letha, and Virginia Ramey Mollenkott, *Is the Homosexual My Neighbor?* (San Francisco: HarperCollins, 1994).

Schaeffer, Francis, *The God Who Is There.* The Complete Works of Francis Schaeffer, Vol. 1 (Wheaton, Ill.: Crossway Books, 1982).

Scroggs, Robin, *The New Testament and Homosexuality* (Minneapolis: Fortress Press, 1983).

Seow, Choon-Leong, ed., *Homosexuality and Christian Community* (Louisville: Westminster John Knox Press, 1996).

Thesaurus Linguae Graece CD-Rom.

Turretin, Francis, *Institutes of Elenctic Theology*, trans. George Musgrave Cider; James T. Dennison, ed. (Phillipsburg, N.J.: Presbyterian and Reformed, 1994), vol. 2.

Weber, Joseph C., *Does the Bible Condemn Homosexual Acts?*

Westminster Larger Catechism (1648), questions 150 and 151.

White, James vs. Barry Lynn, "Is Homosexuality Consistent With Biblical Christianity?" May 24, 2001, Huntington, Long Island, N.Y.

Wilson, Douglas, sermon series on the Ten Commandments.

———. *Fidelity* (Moscow, Ida.: Canon Press, 1999).

Recommended Reading

Are Gay Rights Right? Roger J. Magnusen. Portland: Multnomah Press, 1991.

Fidelity: What It means to Be a One-Woman Man, Douglas Wilson. Moscow, Ida.: Canon Press, 1999.

The Gay Nineties: What the Empirical Evidence Reveals About Homosexuality, Paul Cameron. Franklin, Tenn.: Adroit Press, 1993.

Homosexuality: A Biblical View, Greg L. Bahnsen. Grand Rapids: Baker Book House, 1991.

Homosexuality: Contemporary Claims Examined in the Light of the Bible and Other Ancient Literature and Law, James B. DeYoung. Grand Rapids: Kregel, 2000.

Homosexuality and the Politics of Truth, Jeffrey Santinover. Grand Rapids: Baker Book House, 1996.

Informed Answers to Gay Rights Questions, Roger J. Magnusen. Portland: Multnomah Press, 1994.

Legislating Immoralitity: The Homosexual Movement Comes Out of the Closet, George Grant and Mark A. Horne. Chicago: Moody Press, 1993.

The Pink Agenda: Sexual Revolution in South Africa and the Ruin of the Family, Christine McCafferty and Peter Hammond. Cape Town: Christian Liberty Books, 2001.

Unnatural Affections: The Impuritan Ethic of Homosexuality and the

Modern Church, George Grant and Mark A. Horne. Franklin, Tenn.: Legacy Press, 1991.

When the Wicked Seize a City, Chuck McIlhenny and Frank York. Lafayette: Huntington House Publishers, 1993.

Build Your Faith on the Firm Foundation of Truth

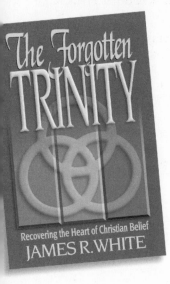

Recovering the Heart of Christian Belief

To be a Christian means to accept and acknowledge the existence of the Trinity, yet many of us are confused and silenced by a doctrine that should offer so much joy. In *The Forgotten Trinity* we are brought back into the presence of the Godhead in a way that will affect how we view God's character and change our worship. Faced with the mystery of the Trinity, we are left with two options: willful ignorance or a deeper understanding of the awesome God that presents himself to us. *The Forgotten Trinity* is a perfect tool for teachers and leaders looking to challenge study groups or congregations, but is equally important for individuals seeking to deepen their understanding of what it means to be a Christian. *The Forgotten Trinity* by James White

Contemporary Answers to Complex Concerns

Are you seeking answers for the difficult questions of life? This comprehensive and readable survey of the central issues of Christianity provides just the conclusive responses readers desire. These answers to the most crucial issues of our time are presented in an easy-to-understand format that helps you remember information for when you'll need it most. With clear and direct evidence, the authors help construct a foundation on which readers may stand firm in this changing world. *Unshakable Foundations* by Dr. Norman Geisler and Peter Bocchino

🜂 BETHANYHOUSE   11400 Hampshire Ave S. Minneapolis, MN 55438
(800) 328-6109 www.bethanyhouse.com

Thank you for selecting a book from
BETHANY HOUSE PUBLISHERS

Bethany House Publishers is a ministry of Bethany
Fellowship International, an interdenominational,
nonprofit organization committed to spreading the
Good News of Jesus Christ around the world through
evangelism, church planting, literature distribution,
and care for those in need. Missionary training is
offered through Bethany College of Missions.

Bethany Fellowship International is a member of the
National Association of Evangelicals and subscribes to
its statement of faith. If you would like further
information, please contact:

Bethany Fellowship International
6820 Auto Club Road
Minneapolis, MN 55438 USA